THE ROYAL ITALIAN AIR FORCE
REGIA AERONAUTICA
1923-1945

The Royal Italian Air Force

Regia Aeronautica

1923-1945

Dr. Spencer Anthony Coil

and

Dr. Renato Zavattini

Schiffer Military History
Atglen, PA

ACKNOWLEDGMENTS

First and foremost the authors dedicate this work to the brave and courageous souls who served in the Royal Italian Air Force or Regia Aeronautica Italiana! You will always be remembered!

Dr. Spencer Anthony Coil would like to begin by thanking his ***Mother, Aunt Frankie,*** and ***Grandmother***. All stood by him and were very supportive in all of his works and endeavors. He is very grateful.

Dr. Renato Zavattini offers great thanks to his family for standing by him during his research.

Furthermore, both authors thank and acknowledge the following individuals who either directly or indirectly assisted in the creation of this work:

Patrick Gariépy (author, historian and consultant)
Ray Charlton (expert, specialist and enthusiast)
Frédéric Gourand (expert, specialist, enthusiast, historian)
Engineer/Diplom Ing. Manyo Manev from Bulgaria (historian, as well as an expert in the fields of historical documents and photos)
The Pomeranzeva-Halikin Family (historians, experts, enthusiasts, linguists, and poets)
Fulvio Rizzo (expert, specialist, enthusiast, historian)
The Hornkohl Family (enthusiasts)
The Otte Family (enthusiasts)
The Ellmauthalers (authors, experts, specialists, enthusiasts, historians)
Alexei Grichine (expert, specialist, and enthusiast)
Dan Eibeck (historian, expert, specialist, enthusiast, archaeologist, analyst, critic, international marketing and public relations liaison)
Professor/ President Del Schwinke
President Dr. David Harpool
President Dr. Wil Goodheer
Vice President Dr. L. Boyer
My Students

A special thanks to internationally acclaimed and recognized military medals and decorations experts, specialists and enthusiasts Herr und Frau Mag. Harmut and Christine Rochowanski, who have maintained an impeccable reputation for over thirty years, and Franz Zabernig and his family.

Finally, a special thanks to the Schiffer team! They are all great to work with, and the books just keep getting better!

Book design by Ian Robertson and Stephanie Daugherty.

Library of Congress Control Number: 2009930322

Printed in China.
ISBN: 978-0-7643-3373-3
We are interested in hearing from authors with book ideas on related topics.

Published by Schiffer Publishing Ltd.
4880 Lower Valley Road
Atglen, PA 19310
Phone: (610) 593-1777
FAX: (610) 593-2002
E-mail: Info@schifferbooks.com.
Visit our web site at: www.schifferbooks.com
Please write for a free catalog.
This book may be purchased from the publisher.
Please include $5.00 postage.
Try your bookstore first.

In Europe, Schiffer books are distributed by:
Bushwood Books
6 Marksbury Avenue
Kew Gardens
Surrey TW9 4JF
England
Phone: 44 (0) 20 8392-8585
FAX: 44 (0) 20 8392-9876
E-mail: Info@bushwoodbooks.co.uk.
Visit our website at: www.bushwoodbooks.co.uk

CONTENTS

PREFACE

A complete history of the Regia Aeronautica, its men, and its methods is outside the scope of this book. Instead, our intention is to present the history of the force and its members in times of peace and in times of war. We have accomplished this by including images from private albums, collections, and archives. We thus believe that this presentation will be all the more interesting, because it will illustrate the human side of this subject. Our intention has not been to present a technical history of this long-overlooked subject, but to present a unique tome that will illustrate the men and the equipment of the Italian Air Force. We hope that, through our choice of photographs, we will be able to convey to the reader the bravery and emotion of those who fought, and to preserve the memory of some of those who died. If the reader comes away with an appreciation for these men, for their suffering and for their sacrifices, then we will have succeeded. Regardless of the cause or country for which he fights, a soldier is too often the one who suffers simply because of his sense of loyalty. At the end of the day they were people just like us, and every one of them deserves to be remembered.

The authors.

INTRODUCTION

A HISTORY OF THE REGIA AERONAUTICA

"We watched with compassionate admiration the gallant Macchi 200 pilots die in their flying crates beside the stukas they had to protect...."

(Rudolf Sinner, Technical Officer of II/JG 27, 1942)

The Birth of the Force and the 1920s

As a result of the sterling service provided by Italian aviators during the First World War, the Regia Aeronautica, or Royal Italian Air Force, was created by Royal Decree n. 645 on March 28, 1923. The decree combined the aerial forces of the army and navy to form a unified air force, just as Great Britain had done with the creation of the Royal Air Force in 1918.

The force's first commander was General Pier Ruggero Piccio. It's newly-designed flag was presented on November 4, 1923, the fifth anniversary of the date on which the Austro-Hungarian Empire, Italy's chief opponent in the war, signed an armistice. On that occasion the Prime Minister Benito Mussolini said:

"We are devoted to a strong aerial policy. All one has to do is to look at a map to see that Italy will never have a sufficient number of aircraft to defend itself."

Thanks to the efforts of Secretary of State for Air Italo Balbo, the fledgling air force developed rapidly in the late 1920s. Aviation schools specializing not only in flying, but also in navigation, etc., were established. In the 1930s, Italian aviators gained international acclaim by setting numerous aviation records, such as timed flights between Europe and North America. Perhaps one of its greatest military accomplishments during this period was the development of strategic bombing theories by aerial strategist Giulio Douhet.

During the 1930s, the Ethiopian Campaign and the Spanish Civil War, aviation schools such as those at Desenzano, Guidonia, Orbetello, and others turned out pilots and aircrew that astonished the world with their accomplishments. With its increase in size, and the improvements in materials and technical advances, the Regia Aeronautica made great strides during its first decade. The opportunity to test its abilities in battle would come in 1936 with the beginning of the Ethiopian campaign. Under the guise of an alleged Somali attack on an Italian garrison and the shooting down of an Italian S.81 transport that was carrying Italian Fascist Minister Razza, Mussolini readied a huge war machine to conquer that East African nation. Fifty-four new airports and airfields were constructed in Somalia, and twenty-eight more were built in Eritrea to the north. They would be required for the five hundred military aircraft employed by the Italians in the region.

The fact that the Ethiopians did not pose any real technological or military match for the Italians meant that the Regia Aeronautica was not really able to test its abilities. It also gave the Italian commanders a false impression of the effectiveness of the force's men, their abilities, their tactics, and their equipment. Nevertheless, the physical challenge of fighting a campaign over such a vast territory, with the extremes of the African climate, did test the mettle of the air force.

The air force was responsible not just for flying combat missions, but also for providing reconnaissance, and for moving men and supplies across its vast area of operations. Initially its squadrons were equipped with Romeo Ro.1 (reconnaissance), Caproni Ca.97 (transport), Caproni Ca.101 (transport), and Fiat Cr.20 (biplane fighter). These aircraft were gradually replaced with the more modern Romeo Ro.37 and Caproni Ca.111 for reconnaissance, and Caproni Ca.133 and Savoia-Marchetti S.81 monoplanes for bombers.

The Spanish Civil War proved to be a more difficult test of the Regia Aeronautica's capabilities. Less than two weeks after the fascist "Caudillo" Francisco Franco declared war on Spain's republican government, Italy unofficially entered the war on the side of the former. She sent in a force of ground troops, the *Corpo Truppe Volontarie* (C.T.V.) "Corps of Volunteers," and units of the

Regia Aeronautica, which they called the *Aviazione Legionaria*, or "Aviation Legion." Initially the aviators were only equipped with nine S.81s, which were three-engine craft that could be used as either a transport or a bomber. However, the numbers employed would quickly rise, and by the end of the 32-month conflict, Italy had contributed 730 aircraft: Bombers (S.81, S.79, Br.20), fighters (Cr.32, Ro.41), ground attack (Ba.65), reconnaissance (Ro.37), and seaplanes (Z.506). The new Fiat G.50 monoplane fighters were also given their initial trial by fire. During the war, Italy's air force flew more than 8,500 war missions.

Without a doubt the Spanish Civil War provided both the Italian and German Air Forces with invaluable information about combat aviation for the coming conflict, and especially value in coordinating fighter and bomber attacks. Unlike the campaign in Ethiopia, both sides employed combat aircraft in Spain, and this gave the Italians (as well as the Germans) the opportunity to truly assess their combat aviation capabilities. However, air combat in Spain was nothing like it would be in the coming world war, and the Italian High Command thus entered war against the Allies with an inflated impression of their air force's equipment and capabilities.

The Second World War

At the beginning of World War II Italy only possessed about 3300 military aircraft. Of this number approximately 1,300 were bombers, 1,100 were fighters, and 800 were reconnaissance aircraft. Of that number only about half of them were operational, and these were deployed over a wide area. Of the Regia Aeronautica's 105,000 personnel, only about 6,300 of them were pilots.

Needless to say, the Regia Aeronautica was both under-equipped and understaffed. Additionally, most of its aircraft were obsolete by then-modern standards, and what aircraft were able to fly were expected to operate on vastly scattered fronts. And even though the technical expertise of the air force's mechanics was high, their abilities were not able to overcome the poor design quality of the aircraft they were expected to maintain. Unfortunately for these men and those expected to operate them in the air, some of the aircraft chosen and the factories at which they were constructed had political motivations behind them. There was little standardization of parts and too many factories were involved in the construction process; as a result production was slow. Between June 1940 and September 1943 Italy only produced 10,400 aircraft. During this same period, the Allies were producing several times this number.

At the beginning of the war, Italy's primary front line fighters were the Fiat Cr.42, which was a biplane, and the Fiat Cr.50 and Macchi MC.200, both monoplanes. All were highly maneuverable, especially the Cr.42, but all lacked the substantial armament of their chief foe, Great Britain. This problem plagued Italian fighters throughout the war, until near the end. And when the problems were finally rectified, it was a matter of too little, too late.

Italy primarily utilized three bombers during the war: the twin-engine Fiat Br.20 and the tri-motor S.81 and S.79. The latter was especially effective as a torpedo bomber. When the war started, the Regia Aeronautica did not have any long-range bombers in its inventory, which impacted its ability to attack behind enemy lines and to attack shipping far out to sea. One such aircraft that did show promise was the Piaggio P.108, nicknamed the "Italian Flying Fortress," but this was introduced in very small numbers only late in the war.

Italian ground assault squadrons only utilized two types of aircraft, both manufactured by Breda. One, the Ba.65, was a single-engine aircraft that was found to be well suited to its task, but the other, the Ba.88, was not. The primary reconnaissance aircraft were the outdated Romeo Ro.37 and the more modern Caproni Ca.311. Reconnaissance units that operated at sea used two different types of seaplane, the Cant Z.501 and Cant Z.506. Transport squadrons primarily used three types of aircraft, the old Caproni and more modern S.81 and S.82.

The battlefronts over which the Regia Aeronautica served were varied and widespread: East Africa, France, North Africa, the Balkans, Russia, and the Mediterranean. It even played a small part in the ill-fated Battle of Britain in 1940. And despite the degree of opposition it faced, the force never caved in. Men and machines fought to the bitter end. From 1940 to 1945, the Regia Aeronautica suffered the loss of 9,000 men killed and 3,500 missing.

When Italy signed an armistice with the western Allies in 1943, the Regia Aeronautica had only a few hundred aircraft left in its arsenal, many of them unable to get off the ground. In 1944 the Allies supplied it with obsolete aircraft, such as the Airacobra and Baltimore, so that it might carry on the war against the Germans. Its pilots and aircrew fought valiantly against its former ally in the Balkans, Albania, Yugoslavia, and Greece. On June 2, 1946, more than a year after the end of the war in the West, a proclamation announced the end of the Regia Aeronautica and the birth of the new Italian Air Force, the Aeronautica Militare Italiana.

While their brethren carried on the fight for the Allied cause, airmen loyal to the Fascist cause fought on for the R.S.I., or Italian Social Republic, as the Aeronautica Nazionale Repubblicana, or Republican National Air Force. This formation, though, is outside the scope of this book.

The Men of the Regia Aeronautica

Throughout the war the Regia Aeronautica experienced difficulty in training new pilots and aircrew. Chronic deficiencies in both aircraft and fuel limited the duration and quality of training, and the result was a lower life expectancy in combat for these brave men.

The Italian pilots were trained differently than were their opponents. In addition to a uniform training doctrine, pilots were put on a pedestal over other aircrew, such as navigators, bombardiers, and gunners. This naturally led to feelings of animosity towards pilots of crew-served aircraft, such as bombers. This was not the case with the Allied air forces, though officers were always given privileges that enlisted men were not. This was service-wide, though, and did not lead to feelings of animosity within single aircrews, which tended to operate as small families.

Fighter pilots' training consisted of three phases: basic, advanced, and operational, all of which were inferior to the training regime of his opponents. Basic training, which lasted nine months, was given at the Scuole di primo periodo or "first period schools," and consisted of about thirty hours on a Breda Ba.25 or a similar aircraft. Later, instruction was given on a more advanced model, such as the IMAM Ro.41. Those who passed their final examinations moved on to the advanced course, or Scuole di secondo period. There, they were given eighty hours of instruction on the Fiat Cr.30, Fiat Cr.32, and models retired from frontline service, such as the Macchi MC.200. The operational training took place when pilots were assigned to their squadrons, where experienced pilots gave them a further thirty hours of time in the air. Squadron or flight leaders would engage the fledgling pilots in finta caccia, which were simulated combats. It was during this phase that pilots got their first experience of learning how to fire at a moving target. In the earlier phases they fired only at fixed targets, such as balloons or objects on the ground.

Like their opponents, Italian pilots excelled at aerobatics, at least those who survived their first few fights. Unlike their foes, Italian fighter pilots often had to do without radio equipment, which required them to fly in tight formations. However, once battle was joined fighter formations quickly split up so the pilots could engage in individual combat. This lack of radio equipment, as well as inferior engines, meant that tactics had to be developed to deal with enemies that were not only better trained but far better equipped, and some Italian fliers excelled at this. If pilots were to survive they had to be especially aggressive: to turn and run from an opponent flying a better designed aircraft with a much more powerful engine was not an option. In North Africa, several Allied pilots reported head-on attacks by Italian Fiat Cr.42 fighters, which they themselves would have considered incredibly reckless.

Like the fighter aircraft of their allies in Japan, Italian planes were light and maneuverable, but short on armor and weaponry. Initially, they were armed only with two 7.7 mm or 12.7 mm machine guns, which were absolutely no match for British fighters, which were armed with eight .303 machine guns.

Even though they were equipped with radios, Italian bombers also flew in tight formations to make up for a lack of armor and defensive weapons. This did little to protect them, though, and many crews were lost in tiny, futile missions. They were no match for either Allied fighters of anti-aircraft guns.

Italian pilots and crews were not rotated out like their American counterparts after a specific number of missions, but continued to fly for as long as they were able.

Tactics

As with all of the world's air forces, aerobatics formed the basis of fighter tactics in the Regia Aeronautica. Squadron and flight leaders developed their own maneuvers, which they added to those taught in the schools to their young pilots. Thus, each squadron might employ different tactics. This was a necessary survival tactic, since Italian pilots almost always flew against adversaries flying more powerful and better-armed aircraft, so it was important that their tactics were unpredictable. While on patrol, pilots generally flew in standard V-formation, in which the patrol leader was flanked by two wingmen, surrounded by more such "Vs."

The Aces

One might wonder why Italian aces were credited with so few victories in comparison to their allies and their opponents. Until 1943, unlike any of the other warring nations, the Regia Aeronautica credited the entire squadron, not the individual, with a victory scored by one of its members. Pilots could only record their victories in their flight logs. As a result, even to this day the tallies of Italian fight pilots are being argued over and updated, and some would argue that victories scored during the Spanish Civil War should not be claimed because they occurred before the Second World War.

Following is a list of Italian fighter pilots that were credited with at least ten victories between 1940 and 1945. Note that this is not a conclusive list of aces, as a pilot must score only five victories to be rated as an ace:

Franco Lucchini	26
Adriano Visconti	26
Teresio Martinoli	23
Leonardo Ferrulli	22
Franco Bordoni-Bisleri	19
Luigi Gorrini	19
Furio Lauri	18
Morosi Luigi	18
Mario Bonzano	17
Mario Visintini	17
Ugo Drago	16
Duilio S. Fanali	15
Adriano Mantelli	15
Luigi Giannella	14
Brunetto di Montegnacco	14
Corrado Ricci	14
Mario Bellagambi	13
Germano La Ferla	13
Vittorio Minguzzi	13
Guido Presel	13
Luigi Baron	12
Giovanni Dell' Innocenti	12
Attilio Sanson	12
Claudio Solaro	12
Gianlino Baschirotto	11
Carlo Magnaghi	11
Angelo Mastroagostino	11
Carlo Romagnoli	11
Carlo Maurizio Ruspoli di Poggio Suasa	11
Pietro Serini	11
Giorgio Solaroli di Briona	11
Ennio Tarantola	11
Mario Veronesi	11
Amedeo Benati	10
Fernando Malvezzi	10
Guido Nobili	10
Giulio Reiner	10
Giuseppe Roberto	10
Massimo Salvatore	10
Giulio Torresi	10

While fighter pilots are given the most attention when it comes to downing enemy aircraft, it is important to remember that crewmen serving on other armed aircraft, i.e. bombers, also scored aerial victories. But we must also remember the men who kept the airplanes flying—the mechanics, armorers, engineers, and fuel and oil specialists. Without them not a single aircraft could have flown. It is to them that every aviator owes his life.

The Regia Aeronautica: The Planes

Unfortunately for the Italian war effort, the production of combat aircraft varied greatly and was sometimes dictated by political considerations. A number of companies contributed designs, most of which paled next to those of their adversaries: Fiat, Macchi, Officine Reggiane, SIAI Marchetti, Breda, Nardi, Cantieri Aero Navali Taranto (CANT), Industrie Meccaniche Aeronautiche Meridionali (IMAM), etc.

Early in the war, Italian aircraft designs were based on maneuverability, with armor and armaments taking a backseat. While these aircraft, which amounted to canvas covering wooden frames, resulted in agile airplanes, it also meant that they were only suited to attack. If they attempted to escape their opponents instead, Italian pilots were quickly overtaken and shot down. Later in the war Italy obtained a license from Germany to build Daimler-Benz engines for its airplanes, which allowed manufacturers to produce aircraft with more power. The Regia Aeronautica was also provided with more and better weapons for its craft.

The following are some of the aircraft employed by the Regia Aeronautica during World War II:

Fighters

Fiat Cr.32 "Freccia" ("Arrow")
Fiat Cr.42 "Falco" ("Hawk")
Fiat G.50 "Freccia" ("Arrow")
Fiat G.55 "Centauro" ("Centaur")
Macchi Mc.200 "Saetta" ("Thunderbolt")
Macchi Mc.202 "Folgore" ("Lightning")
Macchi Mc.205 "Veltro"/"Orione" (Veltro was the greyhound used by the Romans "Orion")
Reggiane Re.2000 "Falco I" ("Hawk I")
Reggiane Re.2001 "Falco II" ("Hawk II")
Reggiane Re.2002 "Ariete" ("Ram")
Reggiane Re.2005 "Sagittario" ("Sagittarius")

Bombers, Torpedo Bombers, and Transports

Savoia Marchetti S.79 "Sparviero" ("Sparrowhawk," but often referred to as "Gobbo" or "Hunchback" by those who flew it)
Savoia Marchetti S.81 "Pipistrello" ("Bat")
Savoia Marchetti S.82 Marsupiale ("Marsupial")
Savoia Marchetti S.84
Savoia Marchetti S.85
Savoia Marchetti S.89
Fiat Br.20 "Cicogna" ("Stork")
Cant Z.1007 "Alcione"
Cant Z.1008 "Leone" ("Lion")
Piaggio P.108
Caproni Ca.111
Caproni Ca.133
Caproni Ca.309 "Ghibli"
Caproni Ca.310 "Libeccio"
Caproni Ca.313
Caproni Ca.314

Idrovolanti/soccorso

Cant Z.501 "Gabbiano" ("Seagull," but referred to as crewmen as "Mammaiut" ("Help me, mother!" and "I'm doomed!"))
Cant Z.506 "Airone" ("Heron")
IMAM Ro.43 (coastal reconnaissance, could be launched from a ship's catapult)
IMAM RO.44 (seaplane fighter)

Ground Assault Aircraft

Breda Ba.65
Breda Ba.88 "Lince" ("Lynx," referred to be crewmen as "Bara volante" or "Flying coffin")

Collegamento "Connection" and Addestramento "Training"

Nardi FN305
Saiman 202
Caproni Ca.164
IMAM Ro.63 (commonly referred to as the Italian "Storch," after the German Fieseler Storch unarmed observation airplane)

The Regia Aeronautica also employed planes of foreign aircraft, primarily from Germany. Examples are the German Messerschmitt BF109 single-engine fighter; the Junkers Ju.87 "Stuka" dive bomber, which Italians called the "Picchiatello"; and the Junkers Ju.88 bomber. Even captured aircraft, such as the French Dewoitine fighter, captured in 1940, were used, and even a few captured American P-38 twin-engine fighters.

Italian aircraft were sometimes utilized by other Axis nations. The Finnish Air Force flew the Fiat G50 on the Russian Front, as did the Hungarian Air Force. On occasion, even the German *Luftwaffe* utilized the S82.

Conclusions

The study of the Regia Aeronautica is a complicated one, but it is possible to arrive at some conclusions. Historians are finally beginning to give the force credit for having fought with gallantry, and the bravery of its pilots and air crewmen is beyond question. This was often remarked on by friend and foe alike, who were often amazed that the Italian Air Force was able to accomplish so much with so little. Lack of radio equipment in many aircraft, a lack of fuel and replacement parts, obsolete airplanes, and a lack of modern aircraft technology did not prevent the men of the Italian Air Force from doing their duty, though all too often at the cost of their lives. The men of the Regia Aeronautica fought until the bitter end and always against stronger opponents. Let us remember and respect their sacrifices.

Both authors would like to thank author and historian Patrick Gariépy for his help and consultation on this introduction. Patrick authored the introduction in *Uniforms and Equipment of the Central Powers in World War I: Volume Two* from Schiffer Publishing, as well.

Chapter One

Aviators and Aircraft

This image displays the front view of a Macchi MC 200. The MC 200 was a fighter aircraft built by *Aeronautica Macchi*. It was also referred to as *Saetta* (Lightning).

Clad in fatigues, this crew poses for a commemorative photo with their biplane parked in a field.

Side view of a Cant Z. (Zappata) 1018 *Leone* (Lion). This is a "pre-series" double tailed aircraft in green (*verde*) camouflage (*mimetic*) paint, which is an ANR color referred to also as *Aeronautica Nationale Repubblicana Colore*.

Rear view of a Cant Z. 1018. The Cant Z.1018 has a wingspan of 73 feet 9 inches (22.5 meters). Both of the images featured on this page are rare.

In this twenties vintage image a crew poses for a commemorative snapshot with their biplane bearing a Scorpio unit marking on the fuselage. Note the flight helmets two of the *Avieri* (Airmen) are wearing. For more detailed images of ancestors to this flight helmet design see *Uniforms and Equipment of the Italian Armed Forces in World War One* by Dr. Coil from Schiffer Publishing.

This image captures a group of Italian soldiers gathered around a biplane. Note the fasces marking on the biplane. Derived from the Latin word *fascis* meaning bundle, a fasces consisted of a bundle of bound wood rods with an ax in the middle.

IMAM (*Industrie Meccaniche Aeronautiche Meridionali*) Romeo Ro. 1 aircraft parked in a field. This aircraft was designed by Fokker and used extensively in Libya.

In this late thirties to early forties vintage image a pilot poses with his Fiat G.8 two-seater biplane. The Fiat G.8 has a wing span of 28 feet 9 inches (8.76 meters) and was usually used for reconnaissance.

This image displays officers of the Regia Aeronautica as well as a Fiat G.8

Regia Aeronautica officers with a Fiat G.8 (left) and a Caproni Ca.164 (right). The Ca.164 was a trainer and had a wingspan of 32 feet (9.75 meters).

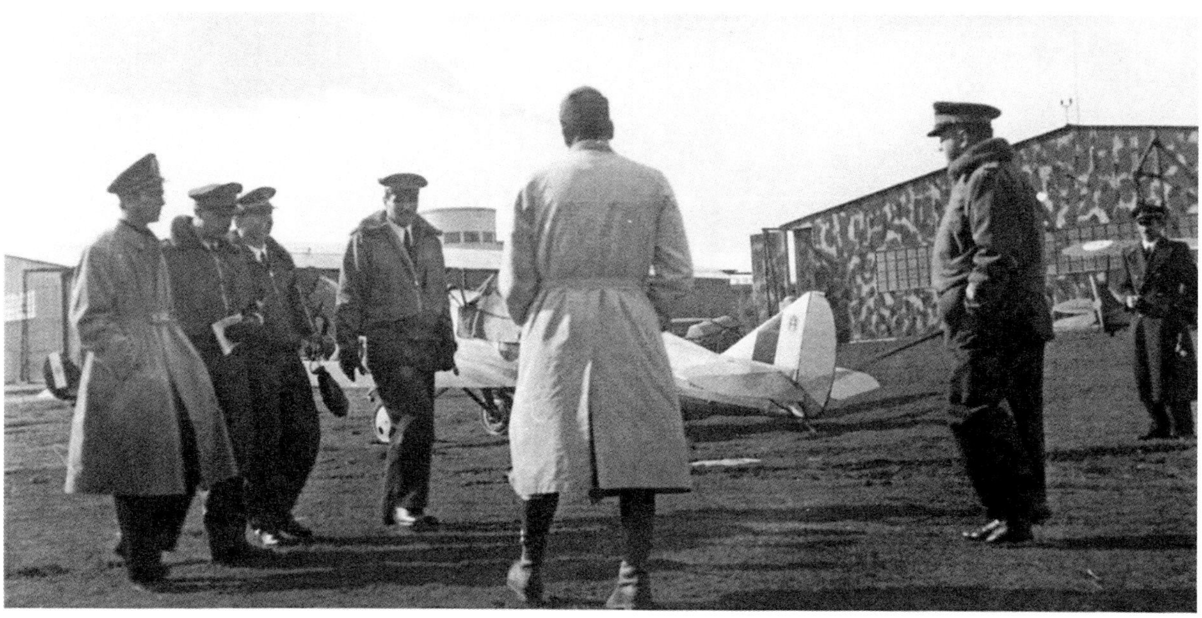

A candid shot capturing Regia Aeronautica officers with a Fiat G.8 (left) and a Caproni Ca.164 (right). (Bottom)

Standing alongside his aircraft, this dark haired pilot poses for a commemorative shot wearing his winter weight flight suit.

Taken from on board a Regia Marina battleship in the Mediterranean, this shot captures what appears to be a Savoia-Marchetti manufactured floatplane/flying boat.

Clad in various styles of headdresses and tunics, this crew poses for a commemorative photo with their biplane parked in a field.

With his hand on the tail section of his biplane, this pilot poses for a photo wearing a summer weight flight suit, necktie, and flight cap with goggles. Note the biplane flying overhead.

This crew poses for a photo with a biplane after a crash landing. Note the fuselage markings. (Top)

This image captures a Fiat BR. 3 light bomber aircraft. This plane has a wingspan of 56 feet 9 inches (17.30 meters). Note the crew wearing summer weight flight clothing.

Wearing his summer weight flight cap, this pilot poses for a photo inside the cockpit of his biplane before takeoff. Note the Regia Aeronautica crest on the tail of the biplane.

This image captures a soldier (*Soldato*) standing in a field watching a Caproni Ca. 100 taxiing. The Ca. 100 has a wingspan of 32 feet 10 inches (10.00 meters) and was used primarily as a trainer.

This image displays a Savoia-Marchetti manufactured floatplane/flying boat coming in for a landing on calm Mediterranean waters.

A rare shot of a Junkers Ju. 88 in *Regia Aeronautica 7th Squadriglia* service. The Ju.88 has a wingspan of 65.88 feet (20.08 meters). For more outstanding images of Ju.88s see pages *217-223* in *Chapter 4* of *Volume Two* in the ongoing series *The German Wehrmacht on all Fronts 1939-1945* from Schiffer Publishing

Another fascinating shot of a Cant Z. (Zappata) 1018 *Leone* (Lion).

Junkers Ju. 88 in *Regia Aeronautica service.*

This image displays a Cansa C. 5 two seat trainer. Designed by Giacomo Mosso and manufactured by *Construtizioni Aeronautiche Novaresi S.A.*, the C. 5 has a wingspan of 27 feet 11 inches (8.50 meters).

Side view of a Cansa C. 5 single seat trainer parked in a field.

Photographed from a unique angle, this image documents a Cansa C. 5 two seat trainer.

This early forties vintage photo displays a Cansa C. 5 single seat trainer parked in a field on the outskirts of a town.

A Cansa C.5 B/1 two seat trainer with an air cooled inverted inline Alfa Romeo 110 engine.

Four Cansa C.5 B/1 two seat trainers with an air cooled inverted inline Alfa Romeo 110 engines parked in a field.

Shot from an unusual position, this photo displays a Cansa C.5 B/1 two seat trainer with an air cooled inverted inline Alfa Romeo 110 engine.

A Caproni Ca. 164 trainer parked inside a hangar.

This thirties vintage image documents a Fiat A.S. 1 in Regia Aeronautica service still retaining civilian markings. The Fiat A.S. 1 was developed in the 1920s and has a wingspan of 34 feet 2 inches (10.40 meters).

This image displays two soldiers with a three engine Caproni Ca. 133 parked on an airfield in East Africa. The Caproni Ca. 133 has a wingspan of 69 feet 8 inches (21.34 meters.

This image captures a Caproni Ca. 133 and crew from the Squadriglia Disperata in an airfield in East Africa. Note the skull and cross bone insignia.

Clad in various styles of uniforms, this group of airmen (*Avieri*) and soldiers (*Soldati*) pose for a commemorative photo with their Caproni Ca. 133. The Ca. 133 was used in the Second Italo-Absyissian/Ethiopian War (1935-1936), Spanish Civil War (1936-1939), and Second World War (1939-1945).

This shot captures what appears to be a Savoia-Marchetti manufactured floatplane/flying boat on calm Mediterranean waters.

A group of soldiers gather around and examine a Ro. 37 of the 103rd Squadriglia R.S. after a crash landing. The Ro. 37 has a wingspan of 36 feet 4 inches (11.08 meters).

General Carlo Pirzio Biroli and his aircraft with fasces and sceptre painted on the fuselage.

This image displays a Caproni Ca. 133 parked at an air base. Note the camouflage pattern.

Taken from inside the aircraft, this photo captures a Cant Z 1007 in flight.

Savioa Marchetti SM.81 three engine bombers from the 213th Squadriglia in flight. The SM. 81 has a wing span of 78 feet 9 inches (24 meters) and is nicknamed *Pipistrello*

Cant Z. 1007 three engine medium bombers in flight. The Cant Z. 1007 has a wingspan of 81 feet 4.5 inches (24.80) and saw action during the Battle of Britain, as well as the Greco-Italian War.

This shot captures in detail the unit insigia painted on the fuselage of a Fiat CR 42 sesquiplane fighter aircraft from the 4th Stormo.

Unit insignia painted on the fuselage of a Fiat CR. 22 *Falco* (Falcon) sesquiplane fighter aircraft from the 4th Stormo. The Fiat CR. 42 was designed by Celestino Rosatelli.

This image displays more unit insignia located on the wheel covers of Fiat CR. 42s of the 4th Stormo.

This image displays more unit insignia located on the wheel covers of Fiat CR. 42s of the 4th Stormo.

This shot captures the crew near a Savoia Marchetti SM. 82 *Marsupiale* (Marsupial). The SM. 82 has a wingspan of 97 feet 4 ½ inches (29.68 meters).

Rear view of a Savoia Marchetti SM. 82 *Marsupiale* (Marsupial) with crew and passengers. The SM. 82 was used as a bomber and transport aircraft. In addition, the SM. 82 had a crew of four and could transport up to forty troops.

One more commemorative photo before boarding.

Crew and passengers pause for a photo before boarding a Savoia Marchetti SM 82 *Marsupiale* (Marsupial).

This image displays not only the grave of an Italian pilot, but also the graves of other soldiers who served in Africa.

The remains of a British Westland Lysander. The Lysander was used primarily as a liason aircraft and could take off from small airstrips.

This image captures an Italian Junker Ju. 87 "Picchiatello" from the 237th Squadriglia (Squadron). For more images of Junkers Ju. 87s see pages 245-49 in Volume Two of *The German Wehrmacht on all Fronts; 1939-1945* from Schiffer Publishing.

A Nardi FN. 305 trainer/liaison aircraft from the 3rd Squadriglia parked at an airbase. The FN. 305 has a wingspan of 27 feet 9 inches (8.74 meters) and was designed by Fratelli Nardi.

Set in the desert near palm trees, this image displays not only the grave of an Italian pilot, but also the graves of other soldiers who served in Africa.

Dressed in an Afrika Korps uniform, this soldier poses for a photo with troops unloading equipment and supplies from two Savoia Marchetti SM. 82 *Marsupiale* (Marsupial) from the 602nd Squadriglia.

Another image displaying troops unloading equipment and supplies from two Savoia Marchetti SM. 82 *Marsupiale* (Marsupial) from the 602nd Squadriglia.

Resting by their equipment with their backs to the camera, these troops watch troops gathered by a Savoia Marchetti SM. 82 *Marsupiale* (Marsupial) from the 602nd Squadriglia.

This is a rare image displaying the insignia of the famous ace Capitano Mario Visintini. Visintini served during the East Africa campaign.

Taken in southern Italy, this image displays a Fiat G. 50 *Freccia* (Arrow) fighter aircraft covered with a protective fitted tarpaulin. Designed by Guiseppe Gabrielli, the Fiat G. 50 *Freccia* has a wingspan of 35 feet 11 inches (10.96 meters).

In this image dated August 21, 1927, six soldiers (*Soldati*) clad in gray green (*grigioverde*) pose for a photo with a BR.1 from the 1st Squadriglia, 13th *Stormo da Bombardamento* parked at the Mirafiori airfield.

Ground personnel and specialists pose for a commemorative photo with their Ro. 1.

Regia Aeronautica and *Luftwaffe* crewmen pose for a commemorative photo with a Macchi MC. 200 *Saetta* (lightning) fighter aircraft undergoing maintenance.

This image displays the graves of pilots and crewman of a downed Italian aircraft. Ridotta Capuzzo, Libya. 1942.

This airman poses atop a downed aircraft. Tobruk, Libya, 1940.

A twin engine Caproni Ca. 313 reconnaissance/bomber aircraft with German unit markings.

Italian paratroops (Paracadutisti) and three Caproni manufactured transport aircraft.

Italian paratroops (Paracadutisti) dropping on an open field.

This image displays crewmen repairing the engine of a Savoia Marchetti SM. 82 *Marsupiale* (Marsupial).

Wearing a summer weight flight cap with goggles, this aviator poses for a photo with a Fiat CR. 32 fighter plane from the 6th *Stormo*.

Wearing his *Cappello* (Italian *Alpini* headdress), this *Alpino* (Mountian trooper) prepares to take photos of aircraft parked near a runway. For further information on *Alpini* (Mountain troopers), see pages 164-179 in Chapter 7 of *Uniforms and Equipment of the Italian Armed Forces in World War One* from Schiffer Publishing.

Dressed in summer attire, this crew poses for a commemorative photo with a partially disassembled Caproni manufactured aircraft near a transport ship at Massaua harbor in east Africa.

This image displays an identified *Maggiore* (Major) *Pilota* (Pilot) of the Regia Aeronautica who piloted a Savoia Marchetti S.79 *Sparviero* (Sparrow-hawk). The S. 79 had three engines and a wingspan of 66 feet 3 inches (20.2 meters).

This image displays a crew putting lubricant in a Caproni Ca. 313.

This Spanish Civil War vintage image displays a mustached Italian pilot and his plane with unit insignia.

This image displays General Messe and a fellow soldier with a Savoia Marchetti SM. 73. The SM. 73 was a three engine transport aircraft with a wingspan of 78 feet 9 inches (24.0 meters).

A candid shot of General Messe smiling as he greets a fellow soldier. Note the pilot and other soldiers as well.

High ranking Italian officers with General Giovanni Messe standing near a Savoia Marchetti SM. 73. General Messe commanded the Italian Expeditionary Corp in Russia (Corpo di Spedizione in Russia or CSIR). Note he has been awarded the Knights Cross or Ritter Kreuz. For more images of Knights Cross wearers see *The German Wehrmacht on all Fronts; 1939-1945* from Schiffer Publishing.

Chapter Two

Various Fronts and Commemorative Shots

This image displays pilots and crewmen from Regia Aeronautica float/seaplanes. Note the various styles of visor caps. (Top)

Pilots and crewmen from Italian float/seaplanes enjoying accordion music.

Another commemorative displaying pilots and crewmen from Italian float/seaplanes enjoying accordion music.

Six pilots and crewmen pose for a commemorative photo with their aircraft. Note the various styles of jumpsuits.

A candid shot of the crew of a CANT (*Cantiere Navale Triestino*) Z. 1007 bis *Alcione* (Kingfisher). The CANT Z. 1007 was a medium bomber powered by three 1000hp Piaggio P.XI radial air cooled engines.

Another candid of the same three crewmen of a CANT Z. 1007 bis *Alcione* (Kingfisher). The CANT Z. 1007 could reach a speed of over 280mph.

This image displays another crewman from the group manning a CANT Z. 1007 bis *Alcione* (Kingfisher). Note the position of the two pockets on the front of his fur collared flight jacket.

A candid shot of more crewmen of a Cant Z. 1007 bis *Alcione* (Kingfisher). Their heavy winter clothing indicates they were stationed on a colder eastern front.

This image displays a crewman working on an engine of a three engine Savoia Marchetti SM. 81 *Pipstrello* (Bat). The SM. 81 operated using Alfa Romeo, Gnome Rhone, or Piaggio manufactured engines.

Pilots and crew clad in winter clothing gathered near Cant Z. 1007 bis *Alcione* (Kingfisher).

This image captures five crew members of a Cant Z. 1007 bis *Alcione* (Kingfisher). The Cant Z. 1007 was armed with either 12.7mm Breda SAFAT or Isotta Fraschini Scotti machine guns. It was armed with 7.7mm Breda SAFAT machine guns as well.

Pilots and crew of a Cant Z. 1007 bis *Alcione* (Kingfisher).

Paracadutisti (Paratroopers) pose for a commemorative photo before embarking on a Savoia Marchetti SM. 82 Marsupiale (Marsupial).

Staring into the sky, this pilot poses for a photo near the tail section of his Cant Z 1007.

This image captures pilots and crew gathered near a Macchi MC. 202 *Folgore* (Thunderbolt) fighter plane parked on a runway. The MC. 202 has a wing span of 34 feet 8.5 inches (10.58 meters).

Another outstanding image of a pilot with his Macchi MC. 202 *Folgore* (Thunderbolt) parked on a runway.

A specialist smiles holding a propeller plane. Eastern front. August 16, 1941.

This image captures a Romeo R. 37bis of the 110th *Squadrigilia* (Squadron) Autonoma in flight over eastern Africa.

This nineteen thirties vintage image displays mechanics pausing for a commemorative shot with their aircraft.

A Macchi MC. 202 *Folgore* (Thunderbolt) parked at an air-base. A MC. 202 could carry 160, 220, or 350lbs bombs (50, 100, or 160 kg).

Dressed in white, this crewman poses for a commemorative with a Savoia Marchetti S. 79. Note the fitted dust covers on the engines.

Italian officers examining the wreckage of an aircraft.

This *Soldato* (soldier) poses for a commemorative shot atop a captured British Bristol Blenheim in Greece. The Bristol Blenheim was a light bomber with a wingspan of 56 feet 4 inches (17.17 meters).

This pilot poses for a commemorative photo with his Fiat CR. 42 *Falco* (Falcon) from the 8th Gruppo in Africa.

An American soldier posing next to a Savoia Marchetti manufactured aircraft after it was shot down.

A Fiat CR. 42 in flight over northern Italy. The CR. 42 could carry a 440lb (200kg) bomb load.

This image captures a German soldier and his vehicle as well as a Savoia Marchetti SM. 82 *Marsupiale* (Marsupial).

This American soldier poses for a commemorative with a Savoia Marchetti manufactured aircraft which was forced to crash land in an open field. Note the large Red Cross marking on the fuselage.

This soldier poses for a photo atop a Savoia Marchetti SM. 79 after a crash landing in Africa.

This monument commemorates the crash of the S.81 of the Italian fascist minister Luigi Razza, which occurred August 9, 1935, in Egypt.

A stunning image of an Italian Fiat CR. 32 in flight during the Spanish Civil War. This particular CR. 32 is from the famous *Squadriglia Asso di Bastoni* (Ace of Clubs). The *Aviazione Legionaria* (Aviation Legion) was dispatched by the Regia Aeronautica to support the Nationalists during the Spanish Civil War.

An outstanding image capturing a Fiat CR. 42 fighter aircraft in flight.

A Macchi MC. 200 *Saetta* (Lightning) fighter plane in flight. The MC. 200 was designed by Mario Castoldi and manufactured by Aeronautica Macchi.

A rare image of a Piaggio 108 C. (*Civile*=Civil).

This pilot poses with his Macchi MC. 202 fighter plane of the 80th Squadriglia (Squadron), February 25, 1943.

This image displays a heavily damaged Reggiane Re. 2001 fighter aircraft with German markings. The Re. 2001 has a wingspan of 36 feet 1 inch (11 meters).

A smiling Duca d'Aosta of the Italian Royal Family wearing his white summer pilot suit poses for a commemorative with another Italian airman.

Five pilots from the 4th *Stormo* pose for a commemorative photo. Second in from the left is the Gold Medal of Valor recipient Gino Passeri, who served during the Spanish Civil War.

The photographer who took this image dated January 28, 1942, described it as "After the darkest night," a S.79 crewman.

Four pilots of the 1st *Stormo Caccia*. Note the differences in their flight suits.

This image displays a Fiat Br. 20 bomber from the Italian CAI (*Corpo Aereo Italiano*) parked on an airfield in Belgium. The CAI was an Italian expeditionary force that supported the German *Luftwaffe* during the Battle of Britain. Note the two men featured wearing German RAD (*Reich-arbeitdienst*) insignia on the sleeves of their overcoats/greatcoats.

An American soldier posing with a Savoia Marchetti SM. 82 *Marsupiale* (Marsupial) that crash landed in a field.

Two *Regia Aeronauctica* airmen pose for a photo with a Fiat BR. 20 parked in the background.

This American soldier poses atop a downed Savoia Marchetti SM. 82 *Marsupiale* (Marsupial).

Taken from a unique angle, this photo documents a section of a Savoia Marchetti SM. 81 *Pipistrello* (Bat).

A Macchi MC. 200 Saetta (Lightning).

This image documents an IMAM Ro. 44 float/seaplane taking off from near an Italian battleship. Designed by Giovanni Galasso and *Industrie Meccaniche e Aeronauctica Meridionali* (IMAN), the Ro. 44 was a fighter aircraft with a wingspan of 38 feet 1 inch (11.60 meters).

High ranking Italian officers near a Savoia Marchetti SM. 81 *Pipistrello* (Bat) parked in field.

A Savoia Marchetti SM. 79 *Sparviero* (Sparrowhawk) torpedo bomber preparing for takeoff. In addition to Italy the SM. 79 was used by Brazil, Croatia, Germany, Iraq, Romania, Spain, and Kingdom of Yugoslavia. The British RAF even used ex-Yugoslavian SM. 79 in the No. 117 Squadron.

Clad in heavy winter clothing, this crew pauses for a commemorative photo with their Savoia Marchetti SM. 81 *Pipistrello* (Bat). This is the first of several images to follow of the same unit stationed on the Russian front at Stalino airfield.

Dressed in winter attire, this crew poses for a photo with a Savoia Marchetti SM. 81 *Pipistrello* (Bat) and other equipment.

This image documents the crew servicing an engine on a Savoia Marchetti SM. 81 *Pipistrello* (Bat). Note two of the crewmen wear a winter fleece headdress resembling a Russian *Papaha*.

This image documents one of the engines of a Savoia Marchetti SM. 81 *Pipistrello* (Bat) fitted with a protective quilted cover. Note the heating device was used to keep the engine from freezing.

Another image taken from a different angle displaying a heating device used to keep an engine of a Savoia Marchetti SM. 81 *Pipistrello* (Bat) from freezing.

A Savoia Marchetti SM. 81 *Pipistrello* (Bat) flying over Italian troops on the march. Libya, December 1941.

This image documents a single engine Breda BA. 65 ground attack bomber flying over Italian troops in Libya in December 1941. The Breda BA. 65 has a wingspan of 39 feet 8.4 inches (12.10 meters).

A Savoia Marchetti SM. 81 *Pipistrello* (Bat)parked in a field.

This image displays a crewman inside the cockpit of a Savoia Marchetti SM. 81 *Pipistrello* (Bat).

This image displays a group of Regia Aeronautica crewmen repairing a Soviet Russian tank. For more outstanding images of captured Soviet armor see Chapter Two in *The German Wehrmacht on all Fronts: 1939-1945 Volume One* from Schiffer Publishing.

This shot captures the crew of an Savoia Marchetti SM. 81 *Pipistrello* (Bat) parked on a barren snow covered field.

A snow covered Savoia Marchetti SM. 81 *Pipistrello* (Bat) parked on a snow dusted field.

In an attempt to further protect the three engines of their Savoia Marchetti SM. 81 *Pipistrello* (Bat) from freezing the crew has surrounded them with a tent.

Once again, the crew of a Savoia Marchetti SM. 81 *Pipistrello* (Bat) thawing out or warming an engine using a heating device.

Regia Aeronautica crewmen using a heating device to warm or thaw an engine.

This shot displays a tent surrounding the nose of Savoia Marchetti SM. 81 *Pipistrello* (Bat). It is possible for some crew members to have camped inside this area as well.

Regia Aeronautica crewmen pose proudly on a captured Soviet tank for a commemorative group photo. Be sure to see Chapter Two in *The German Wehrmacht on all Fronts: Volume One* from Schiffer Publishing for more images of captured Soviet armor!

Regia Aeronautica crewman observing repairs made to a tracked vehicle.

While the winter snow of the Russian front begins to thaw, this group of Regia Aeronautica crewmen pose for a photo with their Savoia Marchetti SM. 81 *Pipistrello* (Bat).

This image displays crewman and a Savoia Marchetti SM. 81 *Pipistrello* (Bat) during the Spring thaw on the Russian front. Note the fuel barrels.

Regia Aeronautica crewman standing in water with fuel barrels and a Savoia Marchetti SM. 81 *Pipistrello* (Bat) in the background.

This image captures Regia Aeronautica crewmen on a thawing runway with fuel containers and a Savoia Marchetti SM. 81 *Pipistrello* (Bat).

A convertible staff parked on a thawing runway. Note the crew and aircraft in the background.

Regia Aeronautica crewmen and a convertible staff car on a thawing runway.

This image displays Savoia Marchetti SM. 81 *Pipistrello* (Bat) parked on a thawing runway.

This image displays a Regia Aeronautica pilot clad in a summer white flight suit and cap with goggles.

This late thirties to early forties vintage snapshot captures four Italian airmen clad in various styles of Regia Aeronautica clothing.

Two dark haired Regia Aeronautica pilots dressed in white summer weight flight suits pose for a commemorative snapshot.

A mustached Regia Aeronautica pilot wearing a visor cap and single breasted wool tunic.

This Regia Aeronautica pilot poses for a commemorative snapshot outfitted in a summer weight flight suit and cap with goggles.

Standing on a barren plain, this dark haired Regia Aeronautica pilot dressed in a white summer weight flight suit poses proudly for a photo with his right hand clenching his flight cap.

This image captures a Regia Aeronautica pilot clad in a white summer weight flight suit. He is standing on the wing of his German built Stuka Junkers Ju. 87 *Picchiatello* dive bomber. For more outstanding images of Ju.87 diver bombers see pages 245-249 in Chapter 4 of *The German Wehrmacht on All fronts: 1939-1945 Volume Two* from Schiffer Publishing.

With his collar up and his hands in his pockets, this Regia Aeronautica pilot poses for a photo dressed in a winter flight suit.

Two Regia Aeronautica airmen pose for a photo wearing their wear winter weight flight jackets.

Dressed in winter weight Regia Aeronautica clothing, these two pilots pose for a commemorative photo.

This Regia Aeronautica airman poses for a commemorative snapshot with a Savoia Marchetti SM. 81 *Pipistrello* (Bat) parked on a runway.

Wearing his flight jacket with fleece collar, this pilot poses for a snapshot with a Savoia Marchetti SM. 81 *Pipistrello* (Bat) parked in the background.

This candid snapshot captures a group of Regia Aeronautica officers wearing various styles of tropical outfits. They are conversing at an airfield in North Africa.

Italian officers at an airfield in North Africa.

This image captures a group of Italian officers at an airfield in North Africa.

This nineteen twenties vintage image displays a Regia Aeronautica airman with four of his friends dressed in civilian clothing.

Wearing in his summer white gala dress uniform, this Regia Aeronautica pilot poses for a photo with his beautiful newlywed bride.

Four jovial Regia Aeronautica airmen.

This image captures three Regia Aeronautica airmen on leave in a town in Greece.

Ten Regia Aeronautica airmen pose proudly for a commemorative wartime photo. Note many wear capes draped over their shoulders.

An outstanding Spanish Civil War image of a pilot and his Fiat Cr. 32 from *Aviazione Legionaria* (Aviation Legion). The Fiat Cr. 32 is a fighter biplane with a wingspan of 31 feet 2 ¼ inches (9.5 meters). Pilots and their Cr.32s saw action during the Spanish Civil War, as well as the Second World War. Note the pilot's face has been obscured to avoid identification.

This image displays two Regia Aeronautica airmen with a Fiat G50 fighter in Turin, Italy in 1940.

This wartime vintage image documents the remains of an Italian manufactured transport aircraft.

A three engine Cant Z. 1007 parked in a field. Cant Z. 1007s were used by Italy, Germany, and Croatia.

Two Macchi MC 200s and an IMAM Ro. 63 parked in an open field in Africa. The IMAM Ro. 63 was an Italian STOL (Short Take Off and Landing) aircraft similar to the German manufactured Fieseler Fi. 156 *Storch* (stork). For images of the Fieseler Fi 156 *Storch* (Stork) see pages 199-201 and 309 in Chapter Four of *The German Wehrmacht on All Fronts: 1939-1945 Volume Two* from Schiffer Publishing.

This captures a Nardi trainer/ liaison plane from the 42nd Squadriglia as well as a Romeo Ro. 1 and two Romeo Ro. 37 planes.

Ten Regia Aeronautica crewmen pose for a commemorative photo with their plane parked inside a hangar.

This image displays Savoia Marchetti SM. 81 *Pipistrello* (Bat) aircraft parked at an airport in Africa.

A Savoia Marchetti SM. 79 *Sparviero* (Sparrowhawk) parked in an open field.

This image taken in Southern Italy displays the rear view of a Savoia Marchetti SM. 81 *Pipistrello* (Bat) as well as Regia Aeronautica crewmen.

A Savoia Marchetti SM. 82 *Marsupiale* (Marsupial) parked at an airbase in Africa.

This image taken in Africa captures an Italian officer wearing a white visor cap and khaki field shirt with shoulder boards.

Two Regia Aeronautica crewmen pose for a commemorative photo at their airbase.

A smiling Regia Aeronautica medical officer.

This flight engineer poses proudly for a commemorative photo. Note the bomber wings as well as his Albanian Front badge.

This Regia Aeronautica pilot wears a tunic with the first model flight eagle above his left breast pocket.

This mustached Regia Aeronautica officer wears a visor cap with stitched insignia and a double breast pocketed wool tunic.

The high ranking officer in this portrait wears a second model flight eagle above the ribbon bar on his tunic. Note the intricate stitching on his visor cap insignia as well.

In this nineteen twenties vintage image, a Regia Aeronautica crewman poses for a commemorative photo with his hands behind his back and his cap cocked to the side. Note this photo is identified.

With visor cap cocked to the side and his hands on his hips, this Regia Aeronautica officer poses for a commemorative photo with his comrades in the background. Note the Spanish Civil War medals above his left breast pocket.

The high ranking pilot in this studio photo has been awarded medals for valor.

In this wartime vintage image, a Regia Aeronautica crewman poses wearing a four pocketed wool tunic. He appears to be clutching white gala dress gloves in his right hand.

This image captures an Italian pilot wearing a uniform from the Spanish Civil War.

This wartime image displays a dark haired Regia Aeronautica pilot with flight eagle insignia above the left breast pocket on his wool tunic.

With his hands resting on his saber, this Regia Aeronautica crewman poses for a commemorative photo wearing his summer white gala dress uniform with sash and aiguillettes.

This wartime vintage photo displays a smiling Sergeant Major with his cap bearing stitched Regia Aeronautica insignia.

In this wartime vintage image, a dark haired Regia Aeronautica pilot wears a Marus flight suit as well; however, he has chosen to remove the fleece collar. Note his goggles and his privately purchased neck scarf.

This Regia Aeronautica pilot poses for a commemorative photo wearing his Marus flight suit. Be sure to see the color gallery for detailed images of a thermal liner for a Marus flight suit.

The Regia Aeronautica pilot in this image wears a white summer weight flight suit and cap with goggles.

In this wartime image, the Regia Aeronautica pilot wears a winter flight suit with fur collar and white summer weight cap with goggles.

The mustached officer in this portrait is an engineer in the Regia Aeronautica, as is evidenced by the insignia on his visor cap.

Standing in front of a shrine displaying the Blessed Virgin Mary, this Regia Aeronautica officer poses for a commemorative photo wearing his uniform adorned with insignia and award decorations.

This image displays a Regia Aeronautica *Aviere* (Airman) clad in a wool tunic and cap with stitched insignia.

This Regia Aeronautica flight sergeant poses proudly for a wedding photo.

This remarkable shot is dated October 1928 and captures the First World War pilot and ace Arturo Ferrarin (left) and famous pilot and fascist party leader Italo Balbo.

This Regia Aeronautica *Aviere* (Airman) poses proudly for a commemorative photo dressed in his white summer weight flight suit.

The Regia Aeronautica unit pilot commander featured here presented this postcard sized photo to one of his *Avieri* (Airmen) as a souvenir. This photo postcard is dated 1933.

This image displays a Regia Aeronautica NCO from the 68th Squadriglia. Note the *Squadriglia* (Squadron) number is located in a circle on his stitched cap insignia.

In this late nineteen twenties to early thirties vintage image, a Regia Aeronautica Aviere (Airman) poses dressed in a four pocketed wool tunic with rank chevron and a depot issued cap with stitched insignia.

A late nineteen twenties to early thirties vintage photo of a mustached Regia Aeronautica *Aviere* (Airman) wearing a wool tunic with stitched insignia on the shoulder straps and forage cap with stitched insignia as well.

This Regia Aeronautica NCO poses for a studio photo wearing a wool visor cap with stitched insignia and a tunic with a first model flight eagle above his left breast pocket.

Regia Aeronautica *Aviere* (Airman) poses proudly in this late nineteen twenties to early thirties vintage studio photo wearing his four pocketed wool tunic and forage cap.

This Regia Aeronautica *Aviere* (Airman) poses proudly for a commemorative photo dressed in his tropical uniform. This photo was taken in Bengasi, Libya, and is dated 1941. For images of Italian soldiers in Libya during the First World War see Chapter 14 in *Uniforms and Equipment of the Italian Armed Forces in World War I* from Schiffer Publishing.

This Regia Aeronautica *Aviere* (Airman) poses proudly for a photo dressed in his white summer weight flight suit. This image is dated March 1941.

In this late nineteen twenties to early thirties vintage image, a Regia Aeronautica *Aviere* (Airman) poses for a commemorative photo clad in four pocketed wool tunic.

In this late nineteen twenties to early thirties vintage image, a Regia Aeronautica *Aviere* (Airman) poses for a commemorative dressed in four pocketed wool tunic with brass buttons and a side cap with stitched insignia.

This highly decorated Regia Aeronautica officer poses for a studio photo dressed in a visor cap and four pocketed tunic.

This Regia Aeronautica General poses for a studio photo wearing his intricately stitched visor cap and wool tunic with award ribbons and flight eagle. Note he has been awarded two medals for valor.

This image captures a smiling Regia Aeronautica *Aviere* (Airman) dressed in a summer weight flight suit.

Three Regia Aeronautica ground personnel clad in fatigues pose proudly for a late nineteen twenties to early thirties vintage commemorative photo.

A spectacular photo of a twin-engine Caproni Ca. 314 from the 4th Squadriglia, 11th Gruppo parked outside of a hangar. The Caproni Ca. 314 has a wingspan of 54 feet 71/2 inches (16.65 meter) and was used during the Second World War as a bomber aircraft carrying up to a 1102 pound (500 kilogram) load. In addition, the Ca. 314 was armed with two 12.7 mm and one 7.7mm Breda SAFAT machine guns.

This image captures a Cant Z. 506 *Airone* (Heron) on still Mediterranean waters. The Cant Z. 506 has a wingspan of 86 feet 11.3 inches (26.50 meters) and is armed with one 12.7 mm and three 7.7mm Breda SAFAT machine guns.

A group of Italian *Soldati* (Soldiers) lined up in front of a two-seat SAIMAN 202 liaison plane. The SAIMAN (Societá Industrie Meccaniche Aeronautiche Naval) 202 has a wingspan of 34 feet 11 ¾ inches (10.66 meters) and was designed by Mario Bottino.

A Squadriglia of Cant Z. 506, August 1940.

This image displays a Cant Z. 506 from the 190th Squadriglia, 86th Gruppo BM with a pre to early war silver paint finish.

The same Cant Z. 506 from the 190th Squadriglia, 86th Gruppo BM with a pre to early war silver paint finish, only this shot reveals the tail of another plane.

An IMAM Ro.43 leaving for a reconnaissance mission, November 1942.

A pre to early war vintage shot of a Fiat Cr.32 with German markings after a crash landing. The Fiat Cr. 32 was used during the Spanish Civil War as well as during the Second World War.

A twin engine, duel fuselage Savoia Marchetti SM. 92 fighter aircraft with German markings parked in a field. The SM. 92 had a wingspan of 47 feet 6 inches (14.5 meters) and was the Italian answer the United States P-38 Lightning.

This image documents a captured Savoia Marchetti S79 with allied markings captured by 145th RAF Squadron at Castelbenito, Libya.

This image documents a Cant Z 1012 parked in a field.

Regia Aeronautica Caproni Ca.311 parked at an airfield shared with German *Luftwaffe*. The Ca. 311 has a wingspan of 53 feet 2 inches (16.20 meters) and was used for reconnaissance and as a light bomber.

This image displays a naval aviator wearing a wool tunic and visor cap. Taranto, Italy, 1931.

An outstanding image documenting a Fiat G.50 *Freccia* (Arrow) fighter with Croatian markings. The Fiat G.50 has a wingspan of 35 feet 11 inches (10.96 meters) and is armed with two 12.7mm Breda SAFAT machine guns.

This image documents Savoia Marchetti SM. 79 *Sparviero* (Sparrow hawk) with bullet holes and battle damage caused by an Allied fighter aircraft.

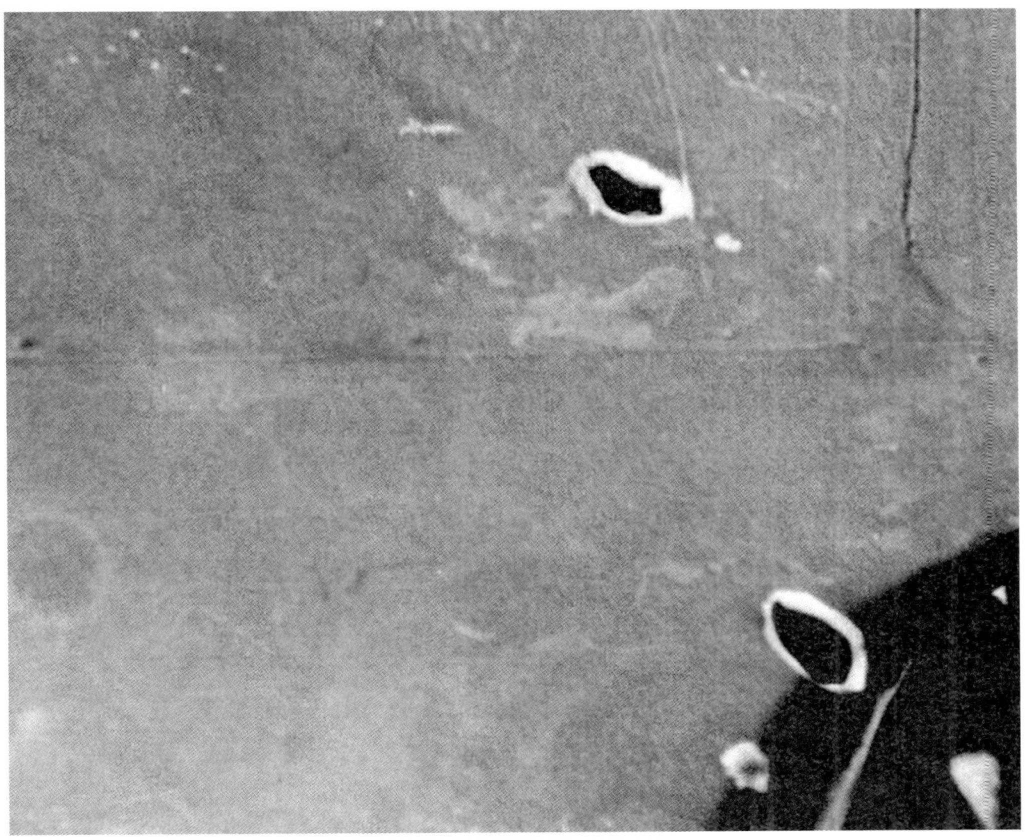

A detail of the bullet holes and battle damage caused by an Allied fighter aircraft.

Chapter Three

Aeronautica Nazionale Repubblicana

An Aeronautica Nazionale Repubblicana 1st Gruppo Caccia: 1st Squadriglia with Macchi MC.205s and 2nd Squadriglia with Messerschmitt Bf 109Gs Vignette

A candid wartime image documenting ANR (*Aeronautica Nazionale Repubblicana*, or the Republican National Air Force) pilot and crew from the 2nd *Squadriglia* servicing a German manufactured Messerschmitt Bf 109 G.

2nd Squadriglia readying for takeoff.

An ANR (*Aeronautica Nazionale Repubblicana*) pilot and crew from the 2nd Squadriglia with a Messerschmitt Bf 109 G. The Bf 109 has a wingspan of 32 feet 6 inches (9.925 meters).

This snapshot documents ANR (*Aeronautica Nazionale Repubblicana*) pilot and crew from the 2nd *Squadriglia* examining the wing of a Messerschmitt Bf 109 G. Note the unit marking.

Two 2nd *Squadriglia* Messerschmitt Bf 109 Gs ready for takeoff. For more images of Messerschmitt Bf 109 fighter aircraft see pages 253-262 as well as 266-282 in *Chapter Four* of *The German Wehrmacht on All Fronts 1939-1945: Volume Two*.

Shot from a unique angle, this photo displays the front portion of a German manufactured Messerschmitt Bf 109 G from the 2nd *Squadriglia*.

Frontal view of a German manufactured Messerschmitt Bf 109 G from the 2nd Squadriglia before takeoff.

Front view of a Messerschmitt Bf 109 G from the 2nd *Squadriglia* parked near a sandbagged position.

This image documents an Italian manufactured Macchi MC. (Macchi Castoldi) 205 *Veltro* (Greyhound) from the 1st *Squadriglia*. Note the open cockpit canopy.

Taken from inside the cockpit, this snapshot captures a line of Macchi MC. (Macchi Castoldi) 205s from the 1st *Squadriglia*. The MC205 has a wingspan of 34 feet 9 inches (10.58 meters).

This image offers a unique perspective of Macchi MC. (Macchi Castoldi) 205s from the 1st *Squadriglia*. Note the crewmen servicing these MC 205s as well.

Three Italian manufactured Macchi MC. (Macchi Castoldi) 205s from the 1st *Squadriglia* parked in a field.

Seven pilots from *Aeronautica Nazionale Repubblicana* 1st *Gruppo Caccia* 1st and 2nd *Squadriglia* relaxing in folding chairs.

Pilots and crew from *Aeronautica Nazionale Repubblicana* 1st *Gruppo Caccia*, 1st and 2nd *Squadriglia* relaxing before a mission.

Pilots and crew from *Aeronautica Nazionale Repubblicana* 1st *Gruppo Caccia* (Fighter Group) 1st and 2nd *Squadriglia* (Squadron) enjoying conversation and a bite to eat. Note the wool service caps with ear flaps some of the men featured here wear. There is one of these caps featured in the color gallery.

A candid snapshot of pilots and crew from *Aeronautica Nazionale* Repubblicana 1st *Gruppo Caccia*, 1st and 2nd *Squadriglia*.

The airbase of *Aeronautica Nazionale Repubblicana* 1st *Gruppo Caccia*, 1st and 2nd *Squadriglia*.

Pilots and crew from *Aeronautica Nazionale Repubblicana* 1st *Gruppo Caccia* (Fighter Group) 1st and 2nd *Squadriglia* (Squadron) discussing plans for their next mission.

This image captures pilots enjoying food and drink. Note how most prefer to wear their life vest even while dining.

A candid snapshot of three ANR pilots. Note the aircraft visible in the background behind the mound.

This snapshot displays an ANR pilot wearing a visor cap with stitched insignia conversing with fellow crew members.

An ANR pilot after a mission.

This dark haired ANR pilot clad in his life vest and flight suit smiles for his commemorative wartime photo.

A profile shot of an ANR pilot wearing his flight jacket with fleece collar and visor cap with stitched insignia.

This image displays an ANR pilot wearing his flight suit, life vest, and visor cap.

This image captures two dark haired ANR pilots smiling.

This snapshot displays an ANR pilot wearing a visor cap with stitched insignia and a belted flight suit with fleece collar.

A dark haired ANR pilot clad in his flight suit and life vest poses proudly for a commemorative wartime photo. Note the detail this image offers on the life vest.

Another commemorative wartime image of a dark haired ANR pilot wearing his fleece collared flight suit and life vest.

This detailed snap shot was taken by an ANR airman and documents unit insignia painted on aircraft. This particular emblem depicts an archer and reads *Incocca tende scaglia* (nocks, pulls, shoots).

This image captures a jovial ANR pilot atop his plane.

This image captures a smiling ANR pilot clad in his fleece collared flight suit and life vest while he rests left arm on his aircraft.

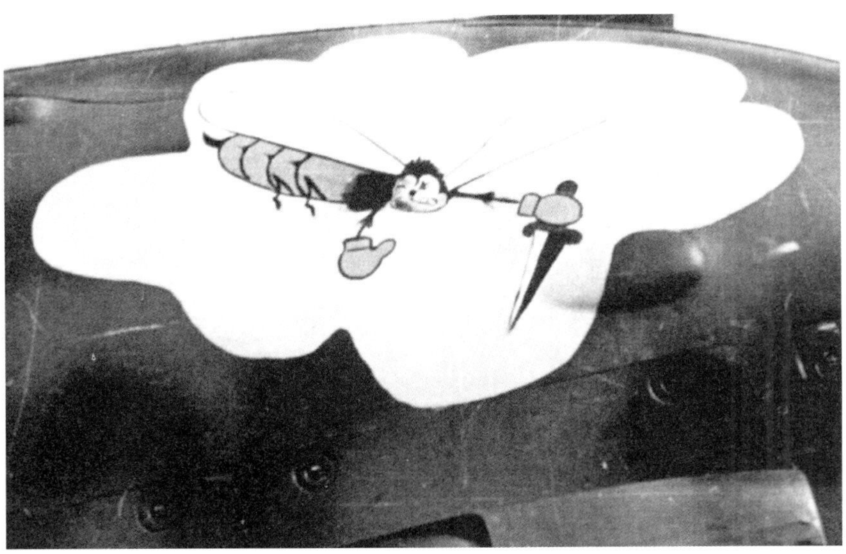

Another detailed snap shot displaying unit insignia painted on aircraft. This emblem depicts a bee or wasp wearing boxing gloves and holding a dagger.

A mustached ANR pilot visualizing air combat using hands.

This ANR pilot clad in his fleece collared flight suit and life vest studies documents while standing near a Macchi MC. (Macchi Castoldi) 205 *Veltro* (Greyhound).

A highly decorated dark haired ANR pilot poses for a commemorative wartime photo with a serious look on his face.

Three ANR pilots clad in fleece collared flight suits and life vests pose for a photo with an Italian manufactured Macchi MC. (Macchi Castoldi) 205 *Veltro* (Greyhound).

ANR airmen standing near their camouflaged Macchi MC. (Macchi Castoldi) 205 *Veltro* (Greyhound).

An ANR pilot clad in his fleece collared flight suit and life vest poses for a commemorative photo near the nose of his Macchi MC. (Macchi Castoldi) 205 *Veltro* (Greyhound).

Two ANR airmen with their Macchi MC. (Macchi Castoldi) 205 *Veltro* (Greyhound).

Three ANR airmen servicing their Macchi MC. (Macchi Castoldi) 205 *Veltro* (Greyhound).

Standing near his Macchi MC. (Macchi Castoldi) 205 *Veltro* (Greyhound), this mustached ANR pilot poses for a commemorative photo with his bambino.

A dark haired ANR pilot with his Macchi MC. (Macchi Castoldi) 205 *Veltro* (Greyhound).

This image captures a dark haired Lieutenant standing near an Italian manufactured Macchi MC. (Macchi Castoldi) 205 *Veltro* (Greyhound).

This image captures a mustached ANR pilot with his Macchi MC. (Macchi Castoldi) 205 *Veltro* (Greyhound) parked under camouflage netting.

Preparing for takeoff.

Two ANR airmen examining the landing gear on their Macchi MC. (Macchi Castoldi) 205 *Veltro* (Greyhound).

Seven ANR pilots from the 1st *Squadriglia* seated on the ground engage in discussion before embarking on a mission.

A candid shot of dark haired ANR pilots with a Macchi MC. (Macchi Castoldi) 205 *Veltro* (Greyhound) in the background.

ANR airmen from the 1st *Squadriglia* engaged in conversation.

Four ANR airmen pose for a commemorative photo with their Macchi MC. (Macchi Castoldi) 205 *Veltro* (Greyhound) parked inside a sandbagged position.

This image documents three unmanned Macchi MC. (Macchi Castoldi) 205 *Veltro* (Greyhound) parked on a rustic airfield.

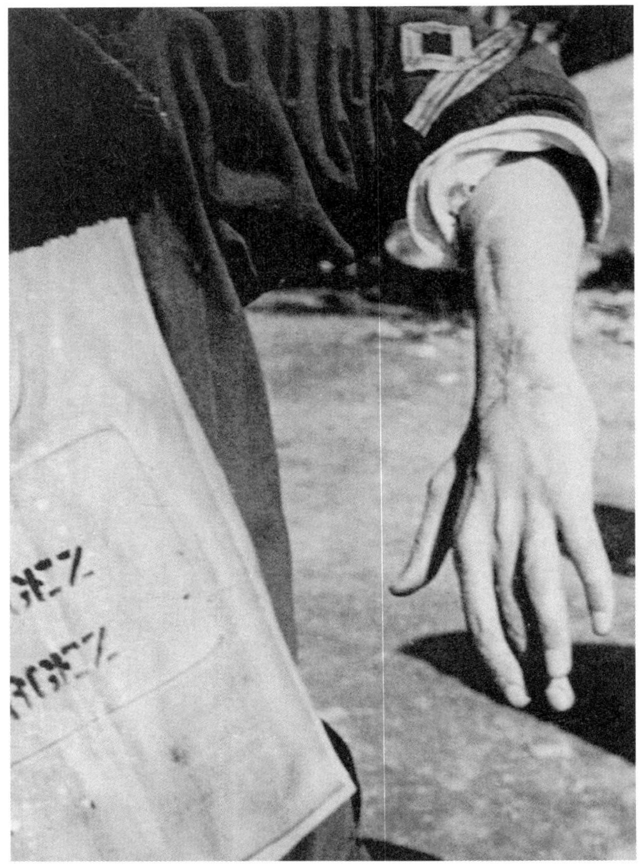

The same ANR pilot using his hand to further express himself. Note a portion of his rank insignia is visible as well.

This ANR pilot wears a fleece collared flight suit with life vest and is using his hand to express himself.

This image documents a camouflaged Messerschmitt Bf 109G.

Seated atop his Messerschmitt Bf 109G, this pilot from the 2nd *Squadriglia* poses for a commemorative wartime photo pointing to his unit insignia.

ANR crewmen from the 2nd *Squadriglia* with their Messerschmitt Bf 109G.

ANR crewmen from the 2nd *Squadriglia* position their Messerschmitt Bf 109G

ANR crewmen from the 2nd *Squadriglia* examine their Messerschmitt Bf 109G. Note the mounting device.

Chapter Four

Unique and Unusual

An Allied soldier observing a partially covered Piaggio P. 108 heavy bomber at an airfield in southern Italy after the invasion.

This image documents a Piaggio P. 108 heavy bomber at an airfield in southern Italy after the Allied invasion. Designed by Giovanni Casiraghi, the P. 108 had a wingspan of 105 feet (32 meters) and is 73 feet 2 inches (22.30 meters) in length.

Regia Aeronautica crewmen preparing a Reggiane Re. 2001 fighter aircraft for action. The Reggiane Re. 2001 has a wingspan of 36 feet 1 inch (11 meters) and two 12.7mm Breda SAFAT machine guns located in the upper cowling, as well as two 7.7 mm Breda-SAFATs located in the wings.

A row of heavily damaged Macchi MC 200 fighter *Saetta* (Lightning) aircraft at an airfield in southern Italy after the invasion. December 24, 1937, marks the first flight of the Macchi MC 200 fighter *Saetta* (Lightning).

This outstanding photo captures a Cant Z. 1007 *Alcione* (Kingfisher) bis bomber of the 261st *Squadriglia* (Squardon) in action over Malta. The Cant Z. 1007 *Alcione* (Kingfisher) has a wingspan of 81 feet 4 ½ inches (24.80 meters) and could carry a bomb load of 4,850 lbs (2200 kg).

This is the first image of thirty-one to follow from a pilot who began with flying CANT (*Cantiere Navale Triestino*) floatplanes and then switched to a CANT bomber unit. This first image displays pilots in a CANT cockpit with a furry friend.

This image documents Cant Z. 506b *Airone* (Heron) floatplanes in flight.

A group of Regia Aeronautica *Avieri* (Airmen) pose for a commemorative photo with a CANT Z. 1007 *Alcione* (Kingfisher) after a forced crash landing.

This Regia Aeronautica *Aviere* (Aviator) has chosen to pose for a commemorative photo atop his CANT Z. 506b *Airone* (Heron) floatplane.

Regia Aeronautica *Avieri* (Airmen) pose for a photo with their CANT Z. 506b *Airone* (Heron) floatplane in the background.

A candid snap shot of Regia Aeronautica crewmen servicing aircraft engines.

Another candid snapshot displaying Regia Aeronautica crewmen installing an aircraft engine.

Regia Aeronautica *Avieri* (Airmen) and Italian *Soldati* (Soldiers) from other branches of the armed forces pose for a group photo.

Another commemorative snapshot of Regia Aeronautica *Avieri* (Airmen) and Italian *Soldati* (Soldiers) from other branches of the armed forces posing for a group photo. Note the mountain trooper, or *Alpino*, on the right.

Two Regia Aeronautica *Avieri* (Airmen) pose for a commemorative photo at their airbase.

This image displays a Regia Aeronautica *Aviere* (Airman) inside the cockpit of his CANT aircraft.

Regia Aeronautica officers on an airbase inspection. Note the crane used to hoist CANT floatplanes from the water.

The crew of a CANT Z. 506b *Airone* (Heron) floatplane decided to inflate their life raft and enjoy a picnic on shore.

Clad in fatigues, these Regia Aeronautica crewmen crowd together for a commemorative group snapshot.

This unique snapshot taken from inside a Regia Aeronautica plane documents a fuel truck filling up captured French manufactured bomber aircraft.

Honoring a valiant Regia Aeronautica *Aviere* (Airman).

Honoring a courageous Regia Aeronautica Aviere (Airman).

This image documents a group of Regia Aeronautica inside a massive hangar housing a CANT Z. 506b *Airone* (Heron) floatplane.

This snapshot documents a speech given inside a hangar to Regia Aeronautica pilots and crew.

Regia Aeronautica crewman servicing an aircraft engine hanging inside a massive hangar.

This image captures five humorous Regia Aeronautica *Avieri* (Airmen) posing for a commemorative snapshot.

The same five Regia Aeronautica *Avieri* (Airmen) posing for a commemorative photo.

A closer shot of the same five Regia Aeronautica *Avieri* (Airmen).

A CANT Z. 1007 *Alcione* (Kingfisher) ready for takeoff.

This Regia Aeronautica crewman poses for a commemorative photo in front of a CANT Z. 1007 *Alcione* (Kingfisher) ready for takeoff.

This image captures two Regia Aeronautica crewman clad in fatigues pose for a photo with bomb load headed to Allied troops.

A CANT Z. 1007 *Alcione* (Kingfisher) after a crash landing. Note the camouflage pattern and unit emblem.

Regia Aeronautica crewman installing an engine on a CANT aircraft.

Four Regia Aeronautica ground personnel pose for a photo with a CANT Z. 1007 *Alcione* (Kingfisher).

These Regia Aeronautica *Avieri* (Airmen) pause for a commemorative photo before boarding his plane.

This image captures five humorous Regia Aeronautica *Avieri* (Airmen) posing for a commemorative snapshot.

This dark haired Regia Aeronautica pilot poses for a commemorative studio photo wearing his Marus flight suit.

A group of Italian aviators pose for a commemorative near their aircraft. Note the insignia resembling skull and crossbones some of these men wear.

This image captures a Macchi MC 200 fighter *Saetta* (Lightning) and crewmen on the Russian Front.

A candid shot of Regia Aeronautica pilots and crewmen near a camouflaged Savoia Marchetti SM. 79 *Sparviero* (Sparrow hawk).

This image displays a group of Regia Aeronautica airmen unpacking supplies near their aircraft.

Africa, 1941.

Italian *Soldati* (Soldiers) celebrating Mass near a camouflaged Savoia Marchetti SM. 79 *Sparviero* (Sparrow hawk).

An airfield in southern Italy, 1940.

This image, which appears to be taken from an elevated position, documents a Regia Aeronautica airbase.

An outstanding image of a Junkers Ju. 87 (Stuka) Picchiatello in flight. Note the white cross on the tail.

A Macchi MC 200 fighter *Saetta* (Lightning) in a sunflower field on the Russian Front.

In this image a Regia Aeronautica officer poses for a wartime studio photo wearing a visor cap with stitched insignia and a four pocketed wool tunic.

A Regia Aeronautica *Aviere* (Airman) poses for a commemorative studio photo. Note the *Moschettieri del Duce* medal he wears on his left pocket.

This wartime photo displays a highly decorated Regia Aeronautica officer.

This Regia Aeronautica *Aviere* (Airman) poses for a commemorative photo with his Macchi racing floatplane on display.

Italo Balbo and Reichsmarshall Goring at Centocelle Airport. 1940.

Greeting a *Regia Aeronautica Squadriglia* (Squadron).

A group of Regia Aeronautica *Avieri* (Airmen/Aviators). Note the M33 helmets with Regia Aeronautica emblems.

Dressed in his white summer flight suit, this Regia Aeronautica *Aviere* (Airman/Aviator) poses for a photo with his two seat Caproni Ca. 164 trainer. The Ca. 164 had a wingspan of 32 feet (9.75 meters).

This image displays a Regia Aeronautica pilot in a Marus flight suit standing in the doorway of his bomber aircraft.

The same pilot from the previous image inside the cockpit of his bomber.

A cloaked Regia Aeronautica cadet pauses for a commemorative photo.

This image documents two Regia Aeronautica *Avieri* (Aviators) going for a stroll.

Three Regia Aeronautica NCOs on leave in Athens, Greece.

This wartime image captures a Regia Aeronautica officer in his staff car in Greece.

A Regia Aeronautica officer standing by his staff car in Greece.

Regia Aeronautica ground personnel building an airstrip pause for a commemorative photo.

This photo displays Regia Aeronautica ground personnel rigorously building an airstrip.

A group of Regia Aeronautica *Avieri* (Airmen/Aviators) pause for a commemorative photo. Note the M33 helmets with Regia Aeronautica emblems.

A group of Regia Aeronautica *Avieri* (Airmen) in Greece. Note the *Aviere* (Aviator) standing in the middle wears a German tropical helmet.

Taken in Greece this image captures a dark haired Regia Aeronautica NCO wearing a tropical uniform and leather belt with holster.

A Regia Aeronautica airman (right) poses for a studio photo with his friend who is in the Italian army (left).

This goateed Regia Aeronautica airman poses for a wartime studio photo wearing his forage cap with stitched insignia and a four pocketed wool tunic.

Eleven Regia Aeronautica *Avieri* (Airmen) pose for a commemorative photo with their canine companion.

A group of Regia Aeronautica *Avieri* (Airmen) pose for a commemorative photo.

Two decorated Regia Aeronautica NCOs pose together for a commemorative studio photo. Note the wound stripe above the chevron on the left sleeve of the NCO standing left.

This decorated Regia Aeronautica NCO pauses in a city for a commemorative photo.

A serious looking Regia Aeronautica officer poses for a studio photo wearing his visor cap with stitched insignia and a four pocketed wool tunic.

This image captures a smiling decorated Regia Aeronautica officer.

This mustached Regia Aeronautica officer poses for a studio photo wearing a four pocketed wool tunic with brass buttons.

A mustached Regia Aeronautica *Aviere* (Airman) wearing a four pocket tunic with decoration ribbon bar.

An image of this Regia Aeronautica officer outdoors.

The same mustached Regia Aeronautica *Aviere* (Airman) wearing a four pocket tunic with decoration ribbon bar. This shot reveals the rank insignia on his sleeves.

This portrait displays a mustached Regia Aeronautica *Avier* (Aviator) wearing a visor cap with stitched insignia and a four pocket tunic with decoration ribbon bar.

Clad in fatigues, this Regia Aeronautica crewman poses for a commemorative photo holding the propeller of his Caproni Ca. 164 trainer biplane.

A Regia Aeronautica *Aviere* (Airman) wearing a white summer weight flight suit poses for a commemorative photo with his plane parked inside a hangar.

This image captures a Regia Aeronautica *Aviere* (Airman) wearing a four pocket tunic with decoration ribbon bar standing inside a hangar.

This late twenties to early thirties vintage image captures seven Regia Aeronautica *Avieri (*Airmen/Aviators) by the burned wreckage of a Fiat CR. 1.

Three Regia Aeronautica NCOs. The right one is the pilot Flight Sergeant Guido Pongiluppi, who is a relative of the author Dr. Renato Zavattini. Pongiluppi was a fighter pilot and was awarded the Bronze Medal of Valor during the Spanish Civil War.

Two Regia Aeronautica *Avieri* (Airmen) and their canine companion pose for a photo near a crash landed IMAM Ro. 37.

This image captures two Regia Aeronautica *Avieri* (Airmen) with a crash landed IMAM Ro.37.

A Regia Aeronautica *Aviere* (Airman) poses for a commemorative photo near an IMAM Ro. 37 after a crash landing.

With his fists on his hips, this Regia Aeronautica *Aviere* (Airman) poses for a photo with his canine friend next to a crash landed IMAM (*Industrie Meccaniche Aeronautiche Meridionali*) Ro. 37.

This image captures a Regia Aeronautica *Aviere* (Airman) wearing a flight suit and parachute preparing to his two seat biplane.

The same pilot almost in his two seat biplane.

This image captures a Regia Aeronautica pilot in training in the cockpit of his plane. Note the RUNA emblem.

Two Regia Aeronautica *Avieri* (Airmen) wearing fatigues and a white summer weight flight suit pose for a photo inside a hangar with their aircraft.

This image captures three Regia Aeronautica NCOs on leave.

This Regia Aeronautica pilot wearing his white summer weight flight suit with rank insignia on the cuffs poses for a commemorative photo near his plane.

Four Regia Aeronautica specialists pose for a commemorative photo. Note their unique uniforms with insignia.

Three Regia Aeronautica specialists pose for a commemorative snapshot near their barracks.

Regia Aeronautica personnel transporting fuel barrels.

Three Regia Aeronautica *Avieri* (Airmen) pause for a commemorative snapshot with their motorcycle.

Another image capturing the same three aviators with their motorcycle.

This image displays four Regia Aeronautica specialists posing for commemorative photo.

This image displays eight Regia Aeronautica *Avieri* (Airmen) wearing four pocket wool tunics and forage caps.

Wearing his gala dress uniform, this Regia Aeronautica *Aviere* (Airman/Aviator) poses for his wedding photo.

This officer wearing a white tunic and ceremonial dress dagger poses for a commemorative shot near the tail section of a Regia Aeronautica aircraft.

Two Regia Aeronautica NCOs wearing overcoats and visor caps going for walk while on leave.

A Ro.1 flying over an Italian camp in Eastern Africa.

This nineteen thirties vintage image displays a group of Regia Aeronautica Avieri (Airmen/Aviators).

Three Regia Aeronautica crewmen clad in forage caps and fatigues pose for a commemorative photo at their barracks.

This wartime image captures four Regia Aeronautica airmen with German built Stuka Junkers Ju. 87 Picchiatello dive bomber. For more outstanding images of Ju.87 diver bombers see pages 245-249 in Chapter 4 of *The German Wehrmacht on All fronts: 1939-1945 Volume Two* from Schiffer Publishing.

Two Regia Aeronautica airmen dressed in wool overcoats and forage caps pose for a commemorative photo.

This group of Regia Aeronautica pilots and personnel pose for a commemorative photo with their floatplane.

A Macchi MC. 200 *Saetta* (Lightning) parked in a field near the front.

The young Luciano Bittante, relative of the author Dr. Renato Zavattini, proudly wears a little Regia Aeronautica officer uniform.

Again, the young Luciano Bittante, who is a relative of the author Dr. Renato Zavattini, proudly wearing a mini-Regia Aeronautica officer uniform.

Another image of young Luciano Bittante, relative of the author Dr. Renato Zavattini, proudly wearing a children's Regia Aeronautica officer uniform.

This candid image captures Regia Aeronautica personnel aboard a transport ship off the coast of Africa.

A group of Regia Aeronautica airmen clad in uniforms and fatigues pose for a commemorative photo. Note the floatplane in the background.

This Regia Aeronautica pilot wearing a Marus flight suit poses for a photo near his plane.

A Regia Aeronautica *Aviere* (Airman) dressed in a white summer flight suit.

High ranking Italian officers on parade. The tall *Regia Aeronautica* officer is the Duca d'Aosta.

A group of Regia Aeronautica airmen clad in fatigue uniforms pose for a commemorative photo.

This is an identified image of a Regia Aeronautica captain.

This studio photo displays a Regia Aeronautica officer wearing a four pocket tunic with necktie.

This snapshot was taken by the rear gunner of a Savoia Marchetti SM. 79 *Sparviero* (Sparrow hawk) and displays the skies over Albania.

Again, a snapshot taken by the rear gunner of the same Savoia Marchetti SM. 79 *Sparviero* (Sparrow hawk) displaying the skies over Albania as well as the Breda SAFAT machinegun.

Another snapshot taken by the rear gunner of the same Savoia Marchetti SM. 79 *Sparviero* (Sparrow hawk) displaying the skies over Albania as well as the Breda SAFAT machinegun.

This image documents a priest blessing a Savoia Marchetti SM. 79 *Sparviero* (Sparrow hawk) in Albania.

An Italian army soldier displaying a device used for visual communication with airplanes using the Morse code alphabet.

Another image from a different angle of a priest blessing a Savoia Marchetti SM. 79 *Sparviero* (Sparrow hawk).

This candid snapshot captures two Regia Aeronautica pilots engaged in conversation at an airbase.t

Regia Aeronautica airmen at an airbase. Note the Savoia Marchetti SM. 79 *Sparviero* (Sparrow hawk) in the background near the camouflaged building.

This image captures Regia Aeronautica arming a Macchi MC200 *Saetta* (Lightning) of the 96th Squadriglia at Brindisi airport, in southern Italy, March 1941.

Crew under the wing of their Savoia Marchetti SM. 79 *Sparviero* (Sparrow hawk) engage in discussion before a mission.

Taken at Brindisi airport, this image documents a Regia Aeronautica crewman belt-feeding a 12.7 mm Breda SAFAT machinegun on a Macchi MC. 200 *Saetta* (Lightning) fighter. March 1941.

Two Regia Aeronautica crewmen arming the 12.7mm Breda SAFAT machineguns on a Macchi MC. 200 *Saetta* (Lightning). Brindisi Airport, March 1941.

Another snapshot of a Regia Aeronautica crewman belt-feeding a 12.7mm Breda SAFAT machinegun on a Macchi MC. 200 *Saetta* (Lightning) parked on a runway at Brindisi airport in southern Italy, March 1941.

Shot from a different position, this image documents a Regia Aeronautica crewman belt-feeding a 12.7mm Breda SAFAT machinegun on a Macchi MC. 200 *Saetta* (Lightning) at Brindisi Airport, March 1941.

This image displays a Fiat G.50 *Freccia* (Arrow) fighter plane of the 154th Gruppo Autonomo CT parked at an Albanian airport.

Two Fiat G.50 *Freccia* (Arrow) fighter planes of the 154th Gruppo Autonomo CT parked at an Albanian airport. Note the pilots and crew visible as well.

Pilots and crew observing Fiat G.50 *Freccia* (Arrow) fighter planes of the 154th *Gruppo Autonomo CT* at an Albanian airport.

Observing Fiat G.50 *Freccia* (Arrow) fighter planes of the *154th Gruppo Autonomo CT* at an Albanian airport.

This detailed image documents unit insignia painted on a Fiat G. 50 *Freccia* (Arrow) fighter plane.

Fiat G.50 *Freccia* (Arrow) fighter planes of the 154th *Gruppo Autonomo CT* parked on the runway at an Albanian airport.

First image in a grouping displaying a pilot wearing a fleece collared flight jacket and shorts from the 92nd *Squadriglia*, 8th *Gruppo CT* standing outside of a dwelling in North Africa.

This Italian ground crewman is servicing a Fiat Cr. 42 *Falco* (Falcon) with the sands of the North African desert blowing about.

Shot from a unique angle, this image documents the covered front portion of a Fiat Cr. 42 *Falco* (Falcon) in North Africa.

With their faces covered to protect from blowing sand, these Italian crewmen work on servicing a Fiat Cr. 42 *Falco* (Falcon).

Italian crewmen wearing protective face gear work on servicing a Fiat Cr. 42 *Falco* (Falcon) in North Africa.

Crew from the 73rd *Squadriglia* preparing a Fiat Cr. 42 *Falco* (Falcon) fighter biplane.
Note this *Squadriglia* (Squadron) share a North African airport with the 92nd *Squadriglia*, 8th *Gruppo CT*.

This Italian crewman wearing protective face gear works on securing a dust cover on one of several Fiat Cr. 42s from the 73rd *Squadriglia* parked at an Italian airbase in North Africa.

The unit's canine mascot.

Two Fiat Cr. 42s from the 92nd *Squadriglia*, 8th *Gruppo CT* in flight.

Two Fiat Cr. 42s from the 92nd *Squadriglia*, 8th *Gruppo CT* shortly before takeoff.

Italian pilots and ground personnel run for shelter while their aircraft are left in the open.

Italian pilots and ground personnel from the 92nd *Squadriglia*, 8th *Gruppo CT*, and 73rd *Squadriglia* run for shelter.

Italian pilots and ground personnel run for shelter.

A commemorative photo is taken after taking shelter. The pilot holding the mascot is the fighter ace Ranieri Piccolomini Clementini Adami from an established noble family.

Three unexploded bombs.

Fighter ace Ranieri Piccolomini Clementini Adami poses with the rest of his unit for a commemorative photo.

Fighter ace Ranieri Piccolomini Clementini Adami.

Front view of a mustached Regia Aeronautica NCO wearing a flight jacket with fleece collar and a privately purchased ascot.

Profile view of a dark haired Regia Aeronautica NCO wearing a privately purchased ascot and fleece collared flight jacket.

A Regia Aeronautica NCO poses for a commemorative photo wearing a pith helmet with insignia and a tropical uniform with rank chevrons on the sleeve of his tunic.

This mustached Regia Aeronautica NCO poses for a commemorative photo wearing a tropical uniform. Note the pith helmet he holds under his left arm.

Three Regia Aeronautica *Avieri* (Airmen/Aviators) in Africa. Each wears a visor cap and shorts.

Three Regia Aeronautica NCOs in Africa.

Three Regia Aeronautica airmen at their barracks in Africa.

Three Regia Aeronautica airmen clad in a variety of clothing pose for a commemorative photo outside of their barracks in Africa.

These two Regia Aeronautica *Avieri* pose for a commemorative photo before boarding their aircraft.

This Regia Aeronautica *Aviere* (Airman) wearing a visor cap and overcoat poses for a commemorative snapshot standing next to a fountain bear amphorae motifs in Italy.

This mustached Regia Aeronautica NCO poses for a commemorative photo at his base.

Wearing a fleece collared flight jacket, this Regia Aeronautica pilot poses for a snapshot at his base.

This mustached Regia Aeronautica NCO poses for a commemorative photo wearing a fitted tunic with decoration ribbon.

With his visor cap tucked under his left arm, this dark haired Regia Aeronautica NCO poses for a commemorative photo with his canine companion.

Eight Regia Aeronautica *Avieri* (Airmen) clad in tropical uniforms pose for a commemorative photo.

The same eight Regia Aeronautica *Avieri* (Airmen) with their hands over their stacked tropical helmets.

A view from inside the cockpit of a Regia Aeronautica aircraft in flight.

This snapshot captures a dark haired Regia Aeronautica NCO inside his barracks quarters wearing tropical clothing.

A mustached Regia Aeronautica NCO wearing a visor cap and barracks clothing poses for a commemorative photo.

This image documents a Regia Aeronautica *Aviere* (Airman) and his floatplane.

This Regia Aeronautica airman poses for a commemorative photo in front of the Fighter Squadron School (*Scuola Caccia Squadriglia*).

A group of Regia Aeronautica *Avieri* (Airmen) pose for a commemorative photo.

A mustached Regia Aeronautica *Aviere* (Airman) poses for a photo with his family.

This image captures two Regia Aeronautica *Avieri* (Airmen) on leave in Italy.

A group of Regia Aeronautica *Avieri* (Airmen) pose for a commemorative photo in ancient ruins.

This is a rare image capturing a Caproni Ca. 111 light bomber and long range reconnaissance aircraft. Designed by engineer Rodolfo Verduzio, the Ca. 111 had a wingspan of 64 feet 3 inches (19.65 meters) and held 2-4 crewmembers. The Ca. 111 could hold up to a 1323lb (600kg) bomb load and has four 7.7mm Breda SAFAT machine guns.

This thirties vintage image displays Regia Aeronautica airmen at Vipacco airport with a Romeo Ro.1.

Another thirties vintage image documenting Regia Aeronautica airmen at Vipacco airport.

A group Regia Aeronautica *Avieri* (Airmen) pose for a commemorative photo at a train station.

This group of Regia Aeronautica *Avieri* (Airmen) clad in wool uniforms and fatigues with a biplane equipped with Isotta Fraschini Asso engines at Vipacco airport.

This is a portrait of a decorated Regia Aeronautica Colonel (*Colonnello*) in gala dress. Note he has been awarded three bravery medals.

Chapter Five

An Italian Aviation Vignette

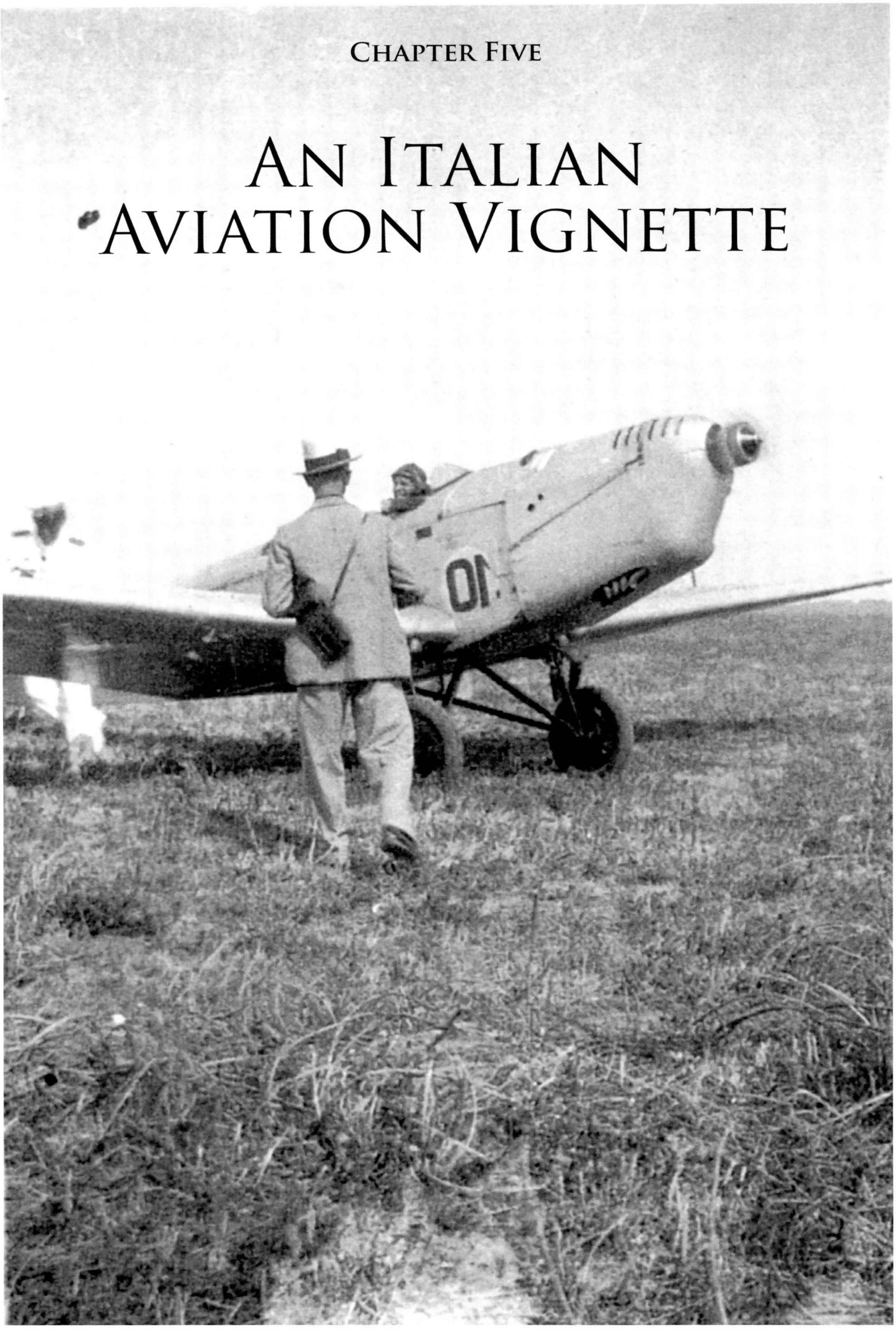

This Regia Aeronautica *Aviere* (Airman) poses for a studio photo wearing a four pocket wool tunic with forage cap bearing stitched insignia. This image is in a photo album and is dated 10-3-1933.

A Regia Aeronautica Bomber Squadron, March 13, 1933.

This image of pilots with their Fiat Cr. 20s in a line commemorates swearing of their oaths of loyalty on April 21, 1932.

This image documents a Caproni Ca. 101 after a crash landing. The Caproni Ca. 101 had a wingspan of 61 feet 8 inches (18.8 meters).

This image dated March 19, 1932, is labeled by the *Aviere* (Airman) featured at the beginning of this chapter "*La Mia Camera*," or "My room."

This photo is labeled by the *Aviere* (Airman) who shot it: "*Formazione Di. B.R. Sul Campo Mirafiori 8-6-1933*" (Formation of BR flying over Mirafiori airfield June 8, 1933).

Eight Regia Aeronautica *Avieri* (Airmen) clad in a variety of barracks clothing pose for a commemorative photo at their base. Note the straw hats.

Regia Aeronautica *Avieri* (Airmen) pose for a commemorative photo with their biplane parked outside a hangar.

Clad in barracks fatigues and wool uniforms, this group of Regia Aeronautica *Avieri* (Airmen) pose for a photo with their biplane parked outside of an aircraft hangar.

This image captures a Caproni Ca. 113 trainer parked in a field. Produced during the nineteen thirties by both Bulgaria and Italy, the Caproni Ca. 113 trainer had a wingspan of 34 feet 5 inches (10.50 meters).

A group of Regia Aeronautica *Avieri* (Airmen) dressed in wool uniforms and cotton fatigues.

Clad in fatigues and wool uniforms, this group of Regia Aeronautica *Avieri* (Airmen) pose for a commemorative photo.

Regia Aeronautica *Aviere* (Airman) in fatigues.

Taken from a unique position, this image documents Regia Aeronautica *Avieri* (Airmen/Aviators) climbing an observation tower.

This image captures four Regia Aeronautica *Avieri* (Airmen) dressed in wool uniforms on leave in town near a monument.

Five Regia Aeronautica *Avieri* (Airmen) pose for a photo with a large aerial bomb by a brick wall.

This image documents two Regia Aeronautica *Avieri* (Airmen) inside a Caproni Ca. 102.

Two Regia Aeronautica *Avieri* (Airmen) dressed in wool uniforms on leave.

Nine Regia Aeronautica *Avieri* (Airmen) pose for a jovial photo dressed in their summer uniforms and straw hats.

Eight Regia Aeronautica *Avieri* (Airmen) pose for a humorous commemorative photo.

In this nineteen thirties vintage studio, a Regia Aeronautica airman poses proudly wearing his wool forage cap with stitched insignia and with star insignia (*Stellette*) on the collar.

Ready for takeoff!

A Regia Aeronautica airman poses for a commemorative with his friend in a suit.

With a serious expression on his face, this Regia Aeronautica airman poses for a nineteen thirties era studio photo dressed in a four pocketed wool tunic and forage cap with stitched insignia.

Regia Aeronautica *Avieri* (Airmen) wearing straw hats form a line for a commemorative photo taken at their airbase.

This image displays a line of Fiat Cr. 1 aircraft from the 2nd *Stormo*.

Eight Regia Aeronautica *Avieri* (Airmen) in a grassy field outside their barracks.

This group of Regia Aeronautica *Avieri* (Airmen) clad in various styles of uniforms pose for a photo with their biplane.

Regia Aeronautica personnel and a IMAM (*Industrie Meccaniche Aeronautiche Meridionali*) Ro.1.

Two Regia Aeronautica airmen pose for a commemorative photo while on leave.

This image captures Regia Aeronautica *Avieri* (Airmen) relaxing in the shade.

This Regia Aeronautica *Aviere* (Airman) poses for a commemorative photo wearing a forage cap and pleated pocketed tunic.

With his hands in pocket, this Regia Aeronautica *Aviere* (Airman/Aviator) dressed in a four pocketed tunic poses for a photo on a dirt road.

Regia Aeronautica airmen wearing white dress gloves pose for a commemorative photo.

This photo was titled by the airman who assembled this album "*Richiamato il 16-7-1935*" (Recalled the 16th of July, 1935).

Regia Aeronautica airmen pose for a commemorative photo with their Fiat Cr. 1.

A Regia Aeronautica airman in civilian dress.

Three Regia Aeronautica airmen dressed in forage caps and fatigues pose for a commemorative photo.

Regia Aeronautica airmen pose for a commemorative photo at a hospital.

A Cr.1 flown by flight sergent Pietro Zorzi after a crash landing. May 27, 1927.

Chapter Six

Various Branches

The Regia Aeronautica officers' mess.

This is an identified image of a Regia Aeronautica flight lieutenant.

Regia Aeronautica officers and civilians. The second from left is the "*Atlantico*" Gallo, which is the pilot who flew one of the airplanes that crossed the Atlantic ocean. Note a pilot's eagle will have the letter *A* on it if he crossed the Atlantic.

This image documents a Savoia Marchetti SM. 79 Sparviero (Sparrow hawk) :axiing on a runway.

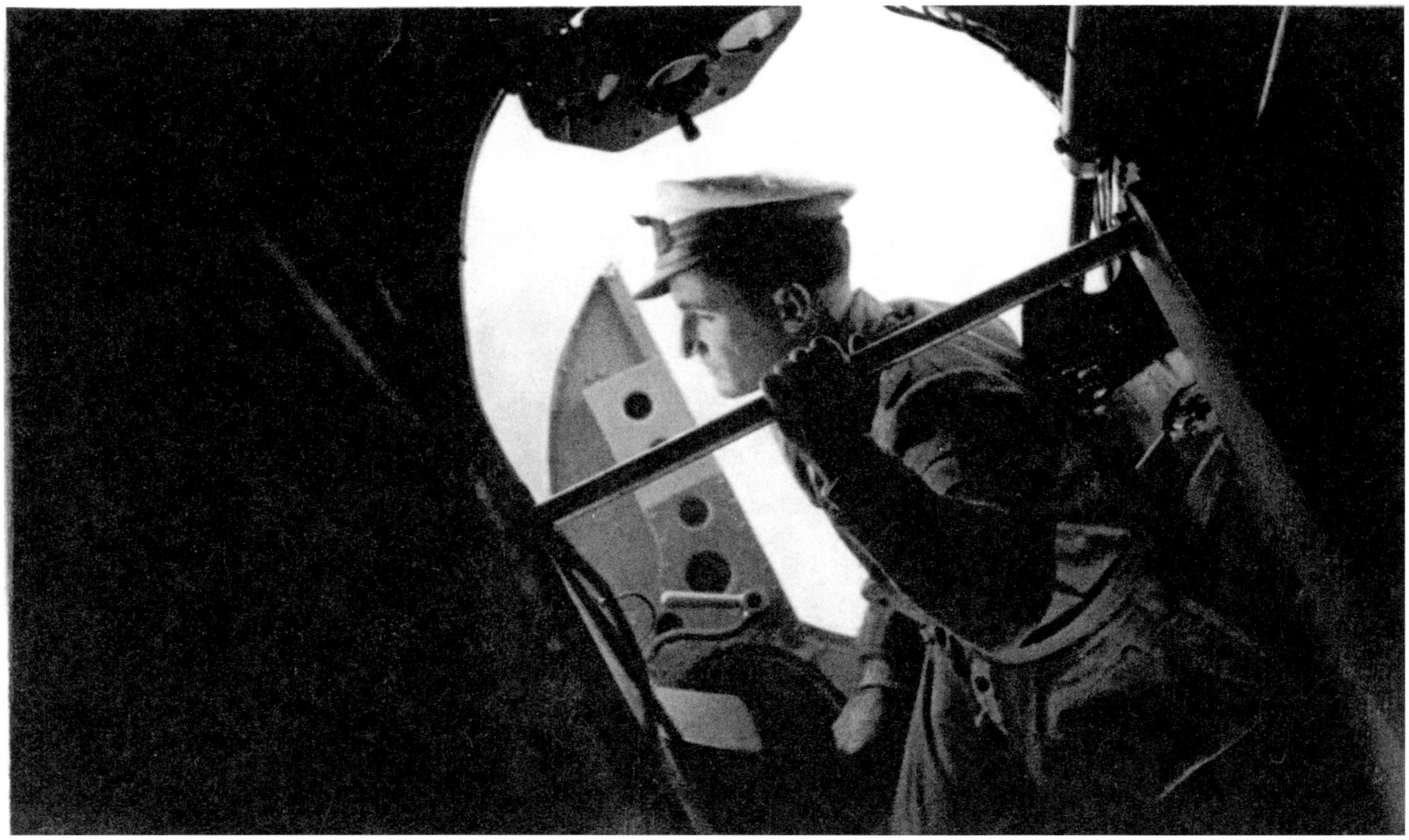

This image captures a Regia Aeronautica *Aviere* (Airman) inside a Savoia Marchetti SM. 79 *Sparviero* (Sparrow hawk).

The gunner inside a Savoia Marchetti SM. 79 *Sparviero* (Sparrow hawk).

Regia Aeronautica personnel servicing a Savoia Marchetti SM. 79 *Sparviero* (Sparrow hawk) before a mission.

Savoia Marchetti SM. 79 *Sparviero* (Sparrow hawk) just landed!

Regia Aeronautica flight lieutenant and personnel near a Savoia Marchetti SM. 79 *Sparviero* (Sparrow hawk). This flight lieutenant is identified on the reverse side of this photo.

A Savoia Marchetti SM. 79 *Sparviero* (Sparrow hawk) parked near an encampment in a lightly camouflaged position.

This image displays a sentry watching a fuel depot.

This image displays tents for Regia Aeronautica crewmen.

Taken from inside a tent, this image documents Regia Aeronautica airmen and two Savoia Marchetti SM. 79 *Sparviero* (Sparrow hawk). A staff car is also slightly visible on the right.

Regia Aeronautica airmen rush to a Savoia Marchetti SM. 79 *Sparviero* (Sparrow hawk) returning from a combat mission.

This image displays Regia Aeronautica airmen rushing to a Savoia Marchetti SM. 79 *Sparviero* (Sparrow hawk) returning from a combat mission.

Regia Aeronautica airmen congratulating each other after a successful mission!

Two Regia Aeronautica airmen pose for a commemorative photo on the porch of their dwelling. Note the Savoia Marchetti SM. 79 *Sparviero* (Sparrow hawk) in the background.

Regia Aeronautica airmen pose for a nineteen thirties vintage commemorative group photo.

Taken in Eastern Africa, this image captures a Caproni Ca.133 flying over an advancing Italian column.

This image displays a Savoia Marchetti S. 66 and crew in Tripoli Harbor, in Libya, in 1936.
The S. 66 is a twin hull floatplane with a wingspan of 108 feet 3 inches (33 meters) and could hold up to 22 passengers.

Four Regia Aeronautica airmen enjoying themselves at a bar on base after having returned from a successful mission.

A Regia Aeronautica floatplane on calm Mediterranean waters.

A Regia Aeronautica floatplane onboard a Regia Marina battleship.

This Regia Aeronautica pilot with the rank of flight sergeant poses for a studio photo wearing a four pocket tunic and visor cap.

Italian soldiers near at the wreck of an enemy plane in Africa.

Two Regia Aeronautica pilots pose with two ladies holding black cats near the Fiat G. 50 *Freccia* (Arrow) belonging to Mario Bonzano, the leader of the 20th Gruppo. Note the unit emblem on the tail depicts a black cat and three green mice.

Taken in Southern Italy, this snapshot captures an Italian pilot of the Squadriglia Buscaglia with his American made Martin 187 Baltimore bomber from the Italian Cobelligerent Air Force.

Seven Regia Aeronautica *Avieri* (Airmen) pose for a commemorative photo. Some of these *Avieri* are holding the toys of the babies for good luck.

This image displays crewmen inside a hangar with Savoia Marchetti SM. 55 floatplane parked inside a hangar at Puntisella airport, near the city of Pola.

This image displays crewmen with a double-hulled Savoia Marchetti SM. 55 floatplane parked on calm waters. Designed by Alessandro Marchetti, the SM. 55 has a wingspan of 74 feet 9 inches (24 meters) and two inline counter rotating propellers.

Recovering a Savoia Marchetti SM. 55 floatplane after a crash.

Savoia Marchetti SM. 55 floatplanes parked outside a hangar at Puntisella airport, near the city of Pola. The first flight of the SM. 55 was in August of 1924.

Regia Aeronautica airmen dressed in fatigues line up near a monument with their rifles for a commemorative photo. Note their straw hats.

This image displays Regia Aeronautica airmen with a Romeo Ro.1 from the 116th *Squadriglia*.

Five Regia Aeronautica airmen from the 66th *Squadriglia* pose for a commemorative photo in the snow near the tail section of their Fiat BR. 20 *Cicogna* (Stork) twin-engine bomber.

Three airmen of the 66th *Squadriglia* with their Fiat BR. 20 *Cicogna* (Stork) twin-engine bomber.
The Fiat BR. 20 *Cicogna* (Stork) has a wingspan of 70 feet 8 ¾ inches (21.56 meters) and could carry a bomb load of up to 3,528 lbs (1600kg).

This image captures five airmen from the 66th *Squadriglia* near Fiat BR. 20 *Cicogna* (Stork) twin-engine bombers.
Fiat BR. 20 *Cicogna* (Stork) twin-engine bombers were each armed with three 12.7mm Breda SAFAT machineguns.

Regia Aeronautica airmen from the 66th *Squadriglia* on top of their Fiat BR. 20 *Cicogna* (Stork) twin-engine bomber. The 66th *Squadriglia* saw action in Yugoslavia.

This image captures high ranking Regia Aeronautica officers speaking with pilots before a mission.

A highly decorated Regia Aeronautica airman decorated poses for a commemorative studio photo. Note the strategic reconnaissance badge on his left breast pocket and the flight engineer badge above his ribbon bars.

This image displays a Regia Aeronautica pilot with a flight badge eagle over his left breast pocket.

This Regia Aeronautica Chaplin poses for a studio photo wearing a visor cap with stitched insignia and a four pocketed tunic with a cross on the left breast pocket.

Regia Aeronautica airmen line up for inspection.

Three Regia Aeronautica pilots pose with a United States P-38 Lightning sold to Regia Aeronautica just after the Second World War ended. The P-38 Lightning has a wingspan of 52 feet (15.85 meters).

Posing for this studio photo is an officer from the commissary (*Commissariato*) branch of the Regia Aeronautica.

This nineteen thirties vintage image displays three Regia Aeronautica airmen clad in wool sweaters and baggy pants standing by their biplane.

Regia Aeronautica crewmen pose for a commemorative photo with their twin-engine Breda Ba.88 *Lince* (Lynx) assault plane. Designed by Antonio Parano and Guiseppe Panzeri, the Ba. 88 has a wingspan of 51 feet 2 inches (15.6 meters).

This image captures German soldiers clad in tropical clothing standing in front of a CANT Z. 506 floatplane. Note the tail of a CANT Z. 501 in the background.

Taken in Sicily, this wartime photo displays German troops in tropical uniforms standing nearing an Italian manufactured three engine Savoia-Marchetti SM.82 *Marsupiale* (Marsupial). The SM. 82 was used as a transport and a bomber and could hold up to 40 troops or 8,800 lb (4000kg) bomb load.

A group of Regia Aeronautica airmen pose for a nineteen thirties vintage commemorative photo.
Note some have chosen to wear their white gala dress gloves.

Regia Aeronautica personnel examining an American made four engine Consolidated B-24 Liberator "Blonde Bomber" after a forced landing. The B-24 Liberator has a wingspan of 110 feet (33.5 meters).

An outstanding image of two Fiat Cr.32 of the 85th fighter squadron (*Squadriglia*) in flight.

Taken in Sicily, this wartime photo displays German troops in tropical uniforms standing nearing an Italian manufactured three engine Savoia-Marchetti SM.82 *Marsupiale* (Marsupial). The SM. 82 was used as a transport and a bomber and could hold up to 40 troops or 8,800 lb (4000kg) bomb load.

An Italian manufactured three-engine Savoia-Marchetti SM.82 *Marsupiale* (Marsupial) at a Sicilian airfield.

Three Italian manufactured Savoia-Marchetti SM.82 *Marsupiale* (Marsupial) parked at an airfield in Sicily.

Taken from a distance, this image documents a Regia Aeronautica transport plane with a camouflage paint scheme.

Regia Aeronautica airmen pose for a commemorative photo with the plane.

This German *Luftwaffe* soldier poses for a commemorative wartime photo with an Italian manufactured Fiat Cr. 42 *Falco* (Falcon). For more detailed images of *Luftwaffe* soldiers and authentic period attire see Chapter Four and the color gallery of *The German Wehrmacht on All Fronts, 1939-1945: Volume Two* from Schiffer Publishing.

Regia Aeronautica airmen pose for a photo with their IMAN Ro.1 from the 115th *Squadriglia*.

This image captures troops near a Savoia-Marchetti SM.82 *Marsupiale* (Marsupial) in North Africa.

Regia Aeronautica *Avieri* (Airmen) in white summer flight suits.

Wearing his flight suit and parachute harness, this Regia Aeronautica *Aviere* (Aviator) poses for a photo with what appears to be a small donkey. Note the shadow of the photographer as well.

This Regia Aeronautica pilot wearing a white summer flight suit and parachute is climbing into a civilian RUNA plane for training.

Taken from inside a plane, this image captures a three engine Caproni Ca. 133 transport/bomber in flight. The Ca. 133 has a wingspan of 69 feet 8 inches (21.34 meters).

This Regia Aeronautica *Aviere* (Airman) dressed in his flight suit poses for a commemorative photo in front of his Breda Ba. 28 trainer, which was often used for acrobatic flying.

Wearing his flight suit and cap with goggles, this pilot with the rank of *Sergente Maggiore* (flight sergeant) poses for a commemorative photo with his aircraft.

The same *Sergente Maggiore* (flight sergeant) walking past a line of Regia Aeronautica biplanes.

Sergente Maggiore (flight sergeant) ready for takeoff!

Clad in a white summer flight suit, this *Sergente Maggiore* (flight sergeant) poses for a photo with his plane.

This is a commemorative photo of a pilot with the rank of sergeant major (*Sergente Maggiore*).

This is an excerpt from an airman's personal log and documents his personal effects.

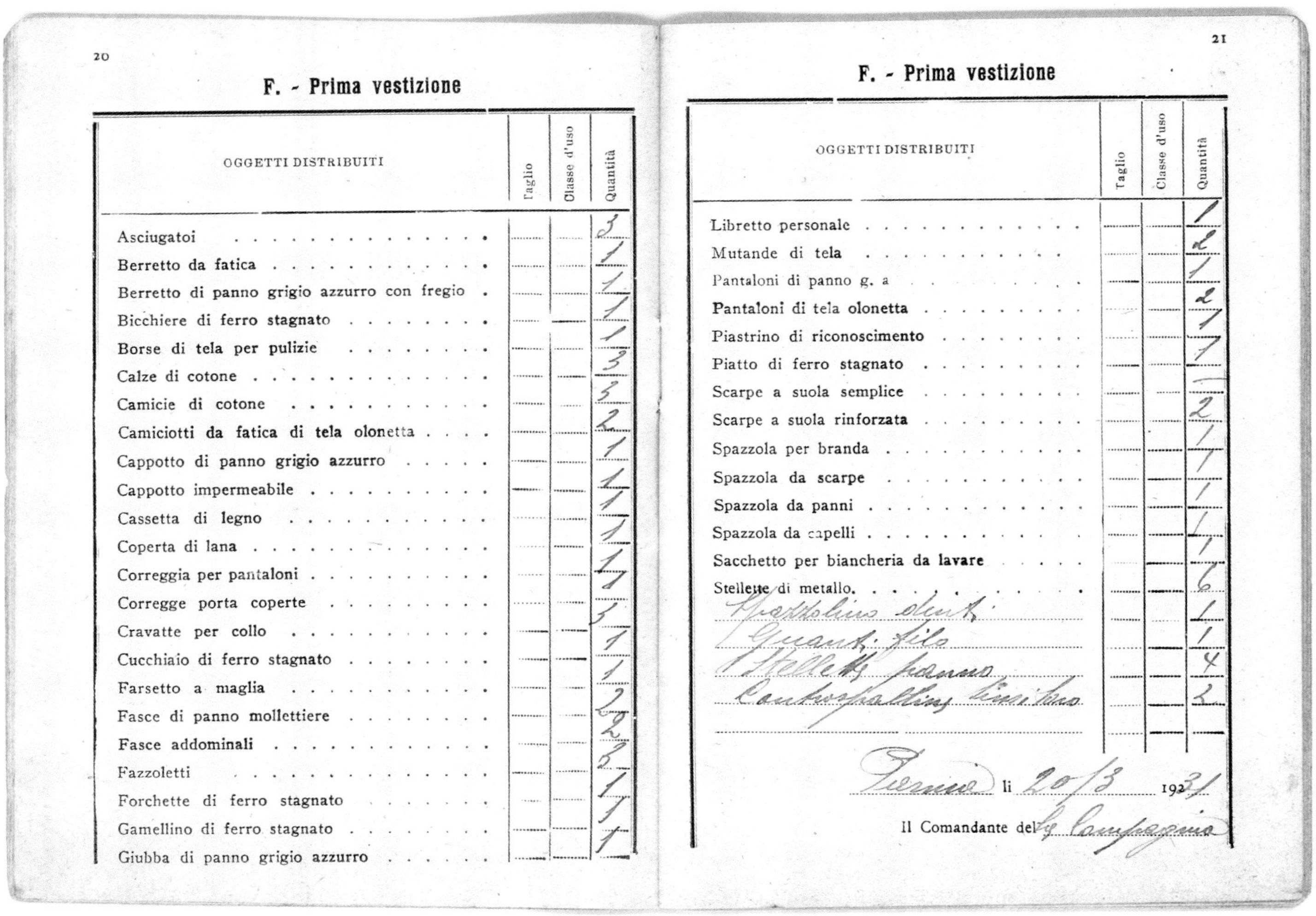

20

F. - Prima vestizione

OGGETTI DISTRIBUITI	Taglio	Classe d'uso	Quantità
Asciugatoi			3
Berretto da fatica			1
Berretto di panno grigio azzurro con fregio			1
Bicchiere di ferro stagnato			1
Borse di tela per pulizie			1
Calze di cotone			3
Camicie di cotone			3
Camiciotti da fatica di tela olonetta			2
Cappotto di panno grigio azzurro			1
Cappotto impermeabile			1
Cassetta di legno			1
Coperta di lana			1
Correggia per pantaloni			1
Corregge porta coperte			1
Cravatte per collo			3
Cucchiaio di ferro stagnato			1
Farsetto a maglia			1
Fasce di panno mollettiere			2
Fasce addominali			2
Fazzoletti			3
Forchette di ferro stagnato			1
Gamellino di ferro stagnato			1
Giubba di panno grigio azzurro			1

21

F. - Prima vestizione

OGGETTI DISTRIBUITI	Taglio	Classe d'uso	Quantità
Libretto personale			1
Mutande di tela			2
Pantaloni di panno g. a			1
Pantaloni di tela olonetta			2
Piastrino di riconoscimento			1
Piatto di ferro stagnato			1
Scarpe a suola semplice			—
Scarpe a suola rinforzata			2
Spazzola per branda			1
Spazzola da scarpe			1
Spazzola da panni			1
Spazzola da capelli			1
Sacchetto per biancheria da lavare			1
Stellette di metallo			6
Spazzolino denti			1
Guanti filo			1
Stellette panno			4
Controspalline lucide			2

Torino li 20/3 1931

Il Comandante del 4 Compagnia

A Romeo Ro.1 of the 41th *Squadriglia* returning home after landing at Debrà Marcòs, Eastern Africa, in 1936.

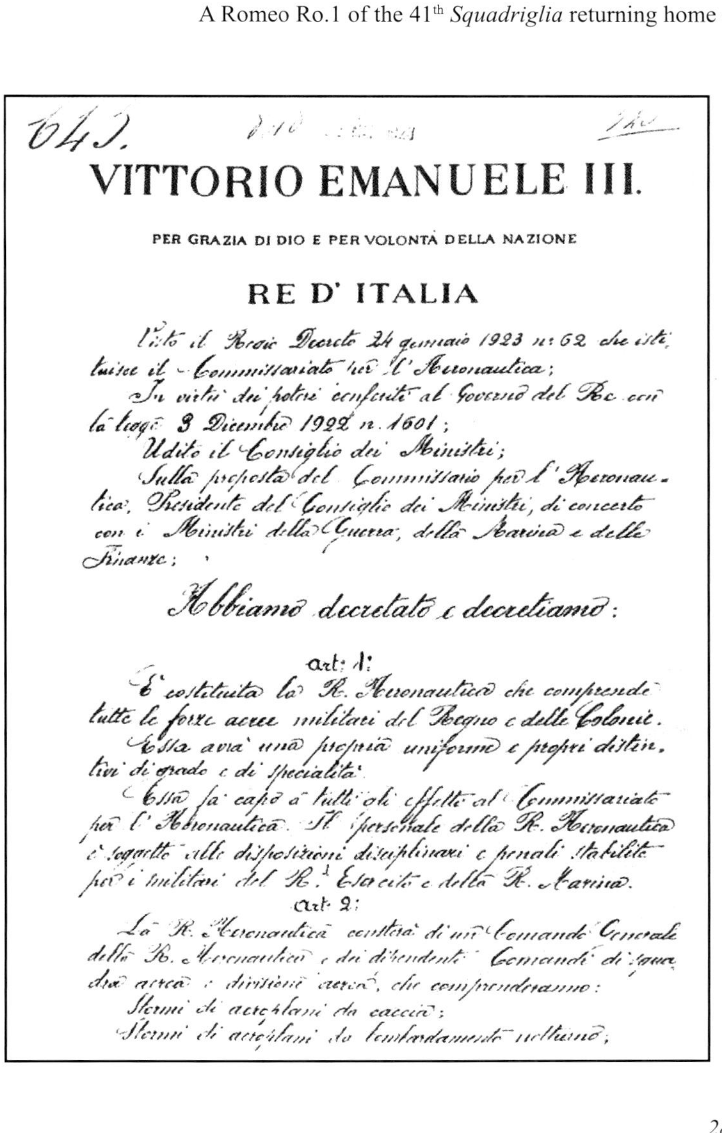

643.

VITTORIO EMANUELE III.

PER GRAZIA DI DIO E PER VOLONTÀ DELLA NAZIONE

RE D' ITALIA

Visto il Regio Decreto 24 gennaio 1923 n. 62 che istituisce il Commissariato per l'Aeronautica;
In virtù dei poteri conferiti al Governo del Re con la legge 3 Dicembre 1922 n. 1601;
Udito il Consiglio dei Ministri;
Sulla proposta del Commissario per l'Aeronautica, Presidente del Consiglio dei Ministri, di concerto con i Ministri della Guerra, della Marina e delle Finanze;

Abbiamo decretato e decretiamo:

art: 1:
È costituita la R. Aeronautica che comprende tutte le forze aeree militari del Regno e delle Colonie.
Essa avrà una propria uniforme e propri distintivi di grado e di specialità.
Essa fa capo a tutti gli effetti al Commissariato per l'Aeronautica. Il personale della R. Aeronautica è soggetto alle disposizioni disciplinari e penali stabilite per i militari del R.° Esercito e della R. Marina.

art: 2:
La R. Aeronautica consterà di un Comando Generale della R. Aeronautica e dei dipendenti Comandi di squadra aerea e divisione aerea, che comprenderanno:
Stormi di aeroplani da caccia;
Stormi di aeroplani da bombardamento notturno;

This documents the birth of the Royal Italian Air Force on January 24, 1923.

This is a postcard made by 54th Gruppo Autonomo BT.

A stunning shot of a camouflaged Macchi C. 202 *Folgore* (Thunderbolt) in flight! Note the pilot as well.

This outstanding image captures a camouflaged Macchi C. 202 *Folgore* (Thunderbolt) in flight.

This image documents a Macchi M.20 parked outside of a hangar.

A Regia Aeronautica pilot in the cockpit of his floatplane on calm waters.

A Reggiane Re. 2005.

This image captures a Reggiane Re. 2002 *Ariete* (Ram) parked at an airfield.

This image displays an Italian manufactured Reggiane 2002 with German *Luftwaffe* markings.

A Caproni Ca. 73.

Regia Aeronautica *Avieri* (Airmen) and a Caproni Ca. 73. Note the other aircraft in flight.

Regia Aeronautica float plane parked near the sea.

This displays Regia Aeronautica *Avieri* (Airmen) with their floatplane parked on calm waters.

A Regia Aeronautica biplane parked at an airbase.

Chapter Seven

A Fighter and Bomber Vignette

A group of decorated Regia Aeronautica officers conversing near a biplane.

A closer shot of the same group of decorated Regia Aeronautica officers.

A candid shot of decorated Regia Aeronautica officers.

Taken from a unique angle, this photo displays Regia Aeronautica officers near a biplane.

Dressed in his flight suit, this Regia Aeronautica pilot poses for a commemorative photo with his Fiat fighter aircraft.

This Regia Aeronautica pilot poses for a photo with his Fiat fighter aircraft.

Clad in his flight gear, this Regia Aeronautica pilot poses for a photo with his Fiat fighter aircraft.

This image displays two Regia Aeronautica pilots near their Fiat fight aircraft.

Ready for takeoff!

This decorated Regia Aeronautica officer poses for a commemorative photos near a building at his airbase.

This images captures a Regia Aeronautica pilot wearing his flight cap and goggles in the cockpit of his plane before takeoff.

This Regia Aeronautica pilot poses for a photo with his Fiat fighter aircraft.

Two Regia Aeronautica pilots dressed in their white summer uniforms near Savoia Marchetti bombers outside a hangar.

Regia Aeronautica *Avieri* conversing with a Savoia Marchetti bomber in the background.

Shot from a unique angle this image displays a Caproni Ca. 310 *Ghibli* visiting the airbase of the Fiat fighters and Savoia Marchetti bombers.

The same aircraft photographed from a different angle.

Regia Aeronautica *Avieri* (Airmen) at their base.

A Regia Aeronautica pilot near his plane looking off to the sky.

A Regia Aeronautica *Aviere* (Airman) standing near his fighter aircraft.

This image displays a Regia Aeronautica *Aviere* (Airman) wearing his flight suit and a portion of his Fiat fighter aircraft.

A Regia Aeronautica pilot in his biplane before takeoff. Note the fasces insignia.

This image displays a pilot in the cockpit of his two seat biplane ready for takeoff.

Regia Aeronautica officer near his Fiat fighter aircraft.

Taken by a Regia Aeronautica *Aviere* (Airman), this photo documents Savoia Marchetti bombers in flight.

Savoia Marchetti bombers in flight.

This image shot by a Regia Aeronautica *Aviere* (Airman) captures Savoia Marchetti bombers in flight.

Savoia Marchetti bombers flying over mountainous terrain.

Savoia Marchetti bombers in flight.

This Regia Aeronautica *Aviere* (Airman) takes another shot as these Savoia Marchetti bombers approach their target.

Color Gallery

Khaki Regia Aeronautica tropical helmet.

Regia Aeronautica pith helmet.

Czech helmet used by the Regia Aeronautica.

Note the stenciled insignia on the front.

Forward and side views of a tropical khaki visor cap with stitched insignia for Regia Aeronautica officers.

Forward, side, and top views of a *Giusti* flight cap with personalized painted unit insignia and a pair of Ratti goggles (*Occhiali*).

Forward and interior views of a Regia Aeronautica blue wool visor cap with early style insignia for officers.

Side and detail views of the featured Regia Aeronautica blue wool visor cap with early style insignia for officers.

Forward, detail, and side views of a white summer weight visor cap with early style insignia for Regia Aeronautica officers.

Frontal and interior views of a Regia Aeronautica blue wool winter service cap for *Avieri* (Airmen/Aviators) stationed in cold and inclement climates, such as on the Russian front (*Fronto Russo*). Note this model of cap existed during the Second World War as well as the Post War period.

Top, side, and rear views of the same Regia Aeronautica blue wool winter service cap for *Avieri* (Airmen/Aviators) stationed in cold and inclement climates. Note this model of cap existed during the Second World War as well as the Post War period.

Exterior and interior views of a Regia Aeronautica blue wool forage cap for enlisted rank *Avieri* (Airmen).

Front and side views of a Regia Aeronautica blue wool forage cap bearing Spanish Civil War insignia. This cap was worn by a Regia Aeronautica officer in the *Aviazione Legionaria* (Aviation Legion) during the Spanish Civil War.

Front and side views of a tropical khaki forage cap for Regia Aeronautica *Avieri* (Airmen/Aviators) of enlisted rank.

Tropical khaki tunic for a flight sergeant (*Sergente Maggiore*). Note the wound bars on the sleeves and the absence of rank chevrons, indicating regulations were not strictly enforced.

Front and detailed views of a fur collared thermal liner for a Marus flight suit. Thermal liners, such as the one featured here, kept *Avieri* (Airmen) warm at high altitudes.

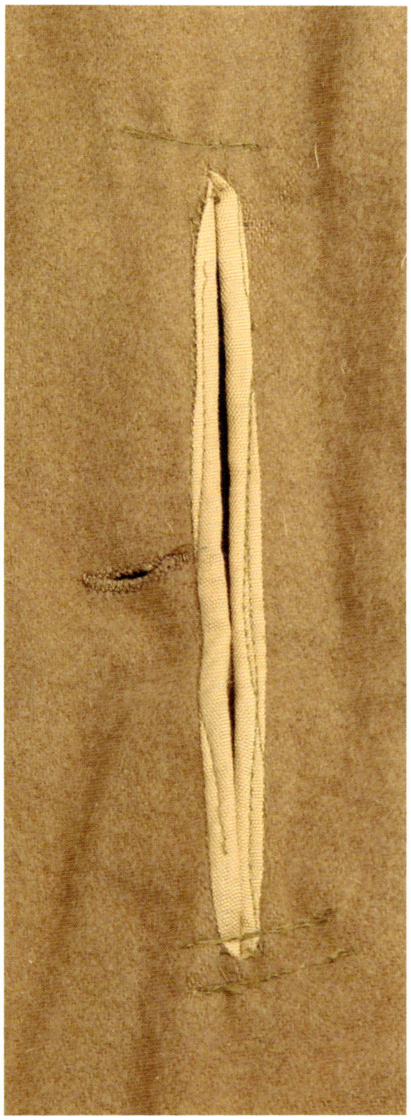

Front and detailed views of a fur collared thermal liner for a Marus flight suit. Thermal liners, such as the one featured here, kept *Avieri* (Airmen) warm at high altitudes.

Frontal and detail views of a black wool gala dress uniform for a pilot ranked second lieutenant (*Sottotenente*) in the ICAF (Italian Cobelligerent Air Force).

Forward and detail views of the Regia Aeronautica tunic of flight sergeant (*Sergente Maggiore*) Boari.

Upper torso and detail views of a Regia Aeronautica blue wool tunic of an engineer (*Genio*) with the rank of captain (*Capitano*).

Upper torso and detail views of a Regia Aeronautica tunic for a flight crewman with the rank of second lieutenant. Note the Albanian Campaign badge above the ribbon bar.

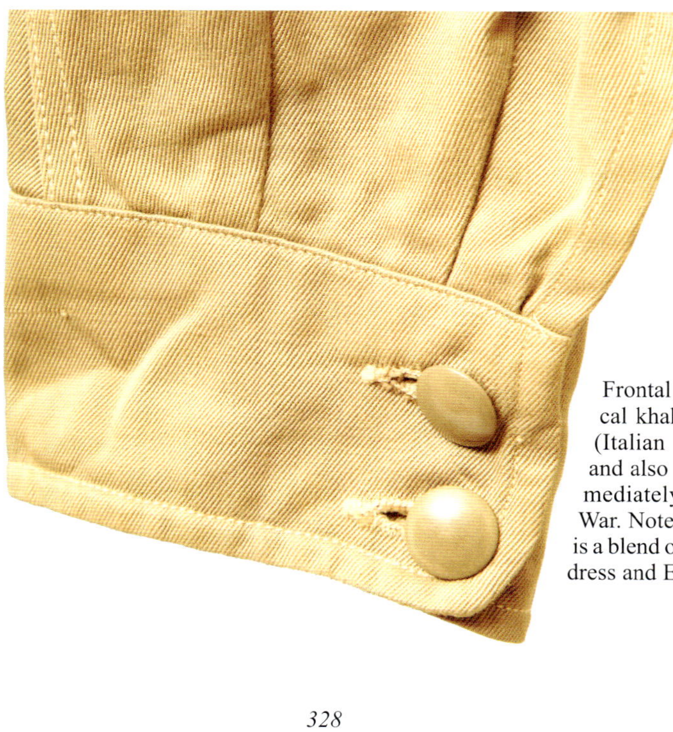

Frontal and detail view of a tropical khaki tunic used by the ICAF (Italian Cobelligerent Air Force), and also the Regia Aeronautica immediately after the Second World War. Note how the style of this tunic is a blend of Italian *Sahariana* tropical dress and English battledress.

Privately purchased tropical khaki shorts for a second lieutenant (*Sottotenente*).

Detailed upper frontal view of a pair of Regia Aeronautica blue wool trousers.

Insignia on a Regia Aeronautica blue wool blanket.

Twelve Regia Aeronautica eagle buttons in original period packaging.

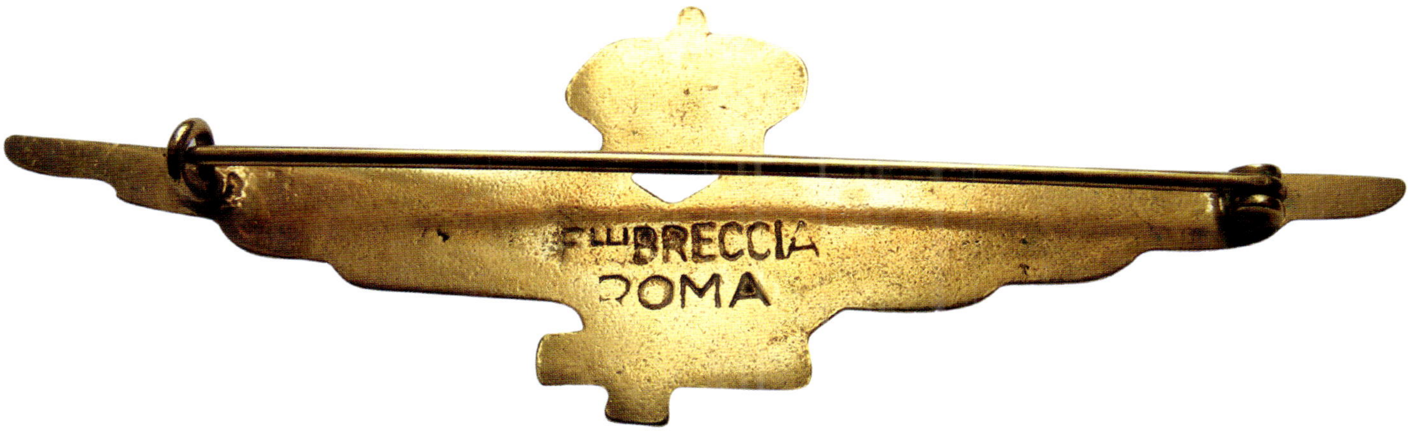

Forward, reverse, and detail views of a gilded Regia Aeronautica pilot eagle.
This particular badge belonged to a sergeant (*Sergente*).

Forward, reverse, and detail views of a gilded Regia Aeronautica pilot eagles.
Note the larger eagle was worn on a combat tunic while the smaller was reserved for gala dress.

Forward, reverse, and detail views of a gilded Regia Aeronautica observer (*Osservatore*) wings.
Note the larger wings were worn on a combat tunic, while the smaller pair were reserved for gala dress.

Flight personnel wings:

Gunner

Flight mechanic

Aerial reconnaissance photographer.

Gilded and enameled badge for *Avieri* (Airmen) in a torpedo bomber unit.

Privately purchased ring for Regia Aeronautica officers.

Shoulder boards and aiguillettes of flight sergeant (*Sergente Maggiore*) Guerrino Boari.

Gilded and enameled badge given to the families of Regia Aeronautica *Avieri* (Airmen/ Aviators) killed in action. Note the symbol of the broken propeller blade.

Gilded and enameled Regia Aeronautica insignia.

The piston of a Macchi MC. 202 *Folgore* (Thunderbolt) fighter aircraft fashioned into a souvenir trench art ashtray to commemorate being stationed in Naples, Italy, during December 1943.

Both sides of a Model 1919 Berretta 6.35mm pistol. This pistol was often carried by Regia Aeronautica *Avieri* (Airmen/Aviators).

Detail shots of the featured Model 1919 Berretta 6.35mm pistol.

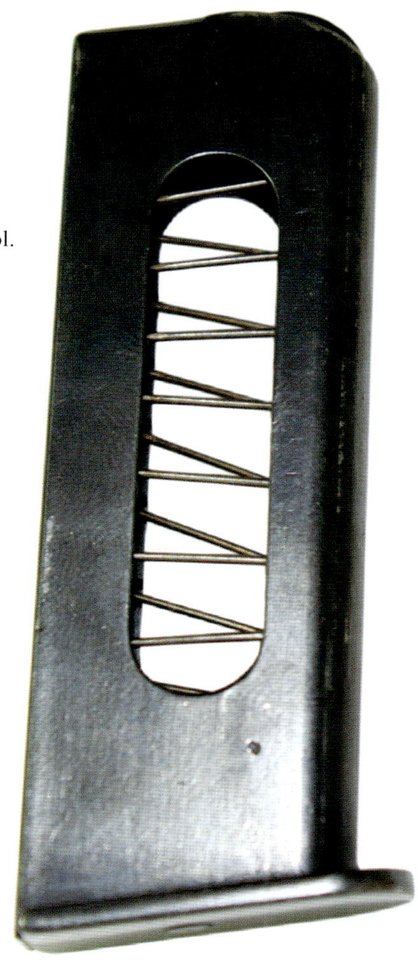

MINISTERO DELL' AERONAUTICA
AVIAZIONE CIVILE
LIBRETTO DI VOLO

STATO CIVILE
Cognome Boari
Nome Guerrino
Paternità Edoardo
Luogo di nascita Bologna
Data di nascita 13 settembre 1917
FIRMA DEL TITOLARE
Roma 15 SET 1937 Anno XV
PEL MINISTRO

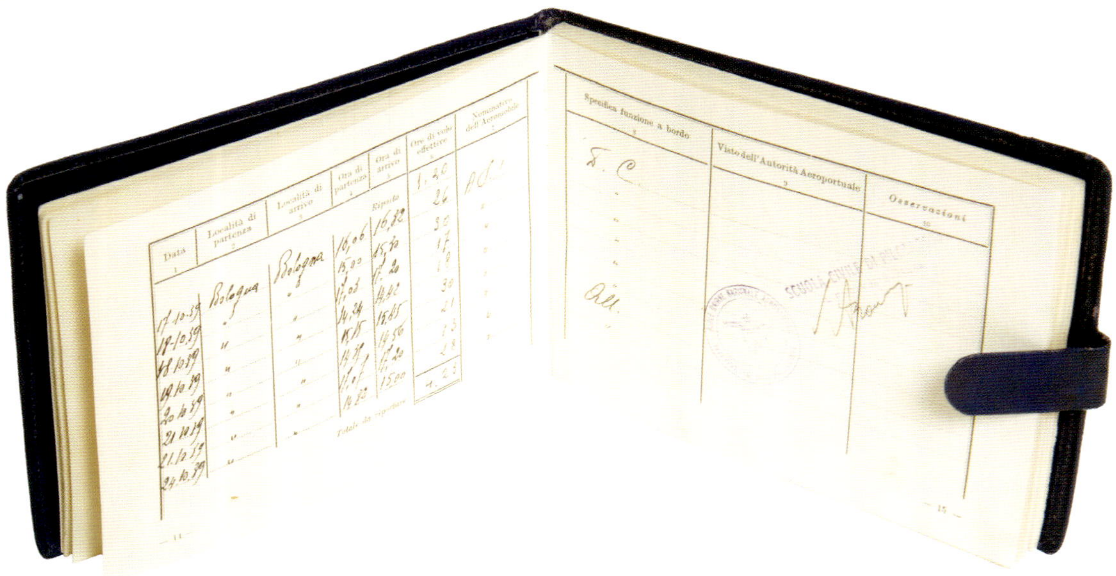
Data
Località di partenza
Località di arrivo
Osservazioni

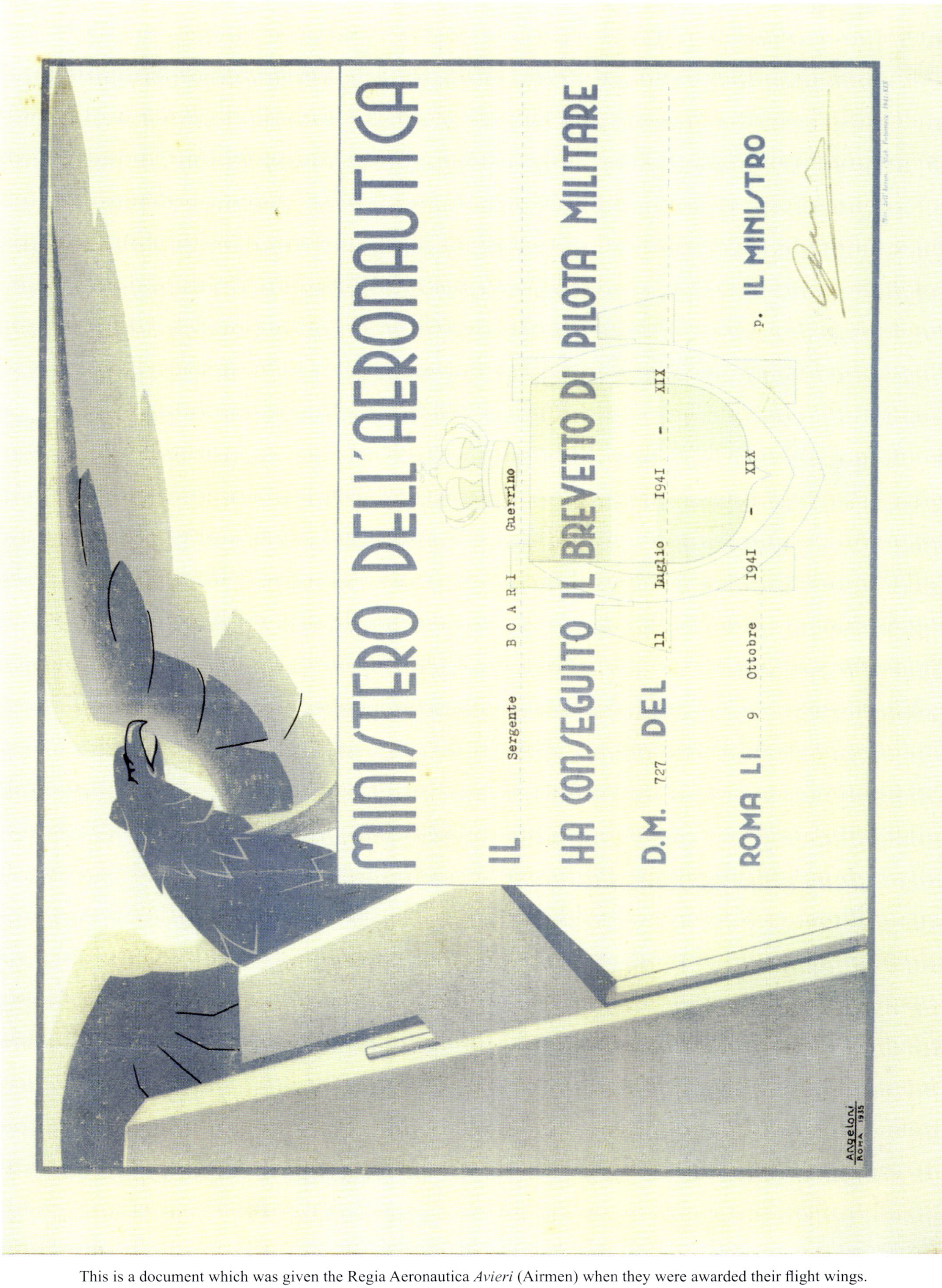
MINISTERO DELL'AERONAUTICA

IL Sergente B O A R I Guerrino

HA CONSEGUITO IL BREVETTO DI PILOTA MILITARE

D.M. 727 DEL 11 Luglio 1941 - XIX

ROMA LI 9 Ottobre 1941 - XIX

p. IL MINISTRO

This is a document which was given the Regia Aeronautica *Avieri* (Airmen) when they were awarded their flight wings.

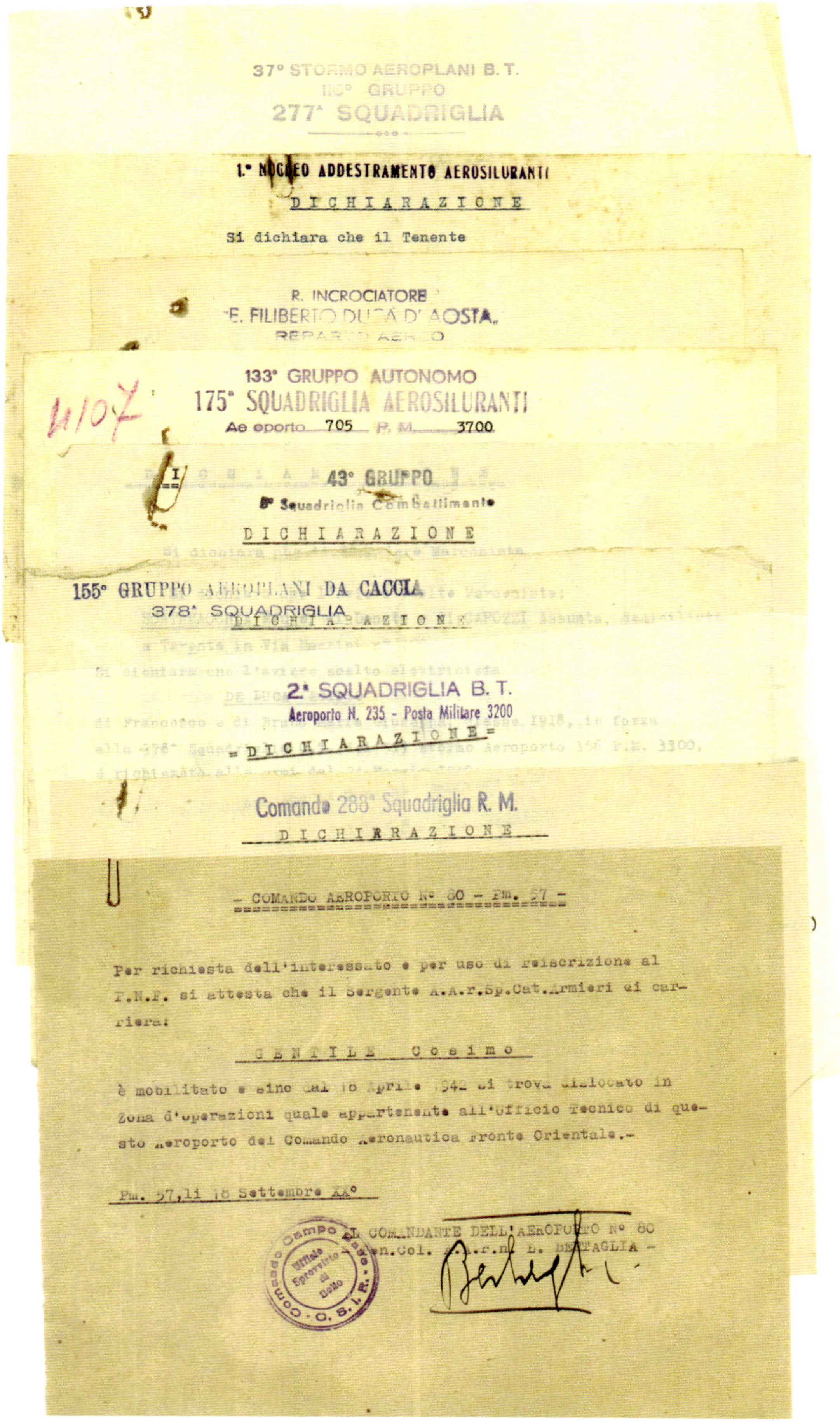

Regia Aeronautica documents with various squadron and unit stamps.

Personal identification booklet of a Regia Aeronautica sergeant (*Sergente*).

Medal of the Madonna di Loreto, the protector of pilots and air personnel.

Personal identification card released in 1940 from the Catania airport in Sicily.

VIAGGI DEGLI IMPIEGATI DELLO STATO E DELLE LORO FAMIGLIE

Regia Aeronautica

~~MINISTERO DELLA GUERRA~~

AVIAZIONE DELLA TRIPOLITANIA

(1) COMANDO

TESSERA PERSONALE DI RICONOSCIMENTO

del la Sig.ra Vita Viginia Chiofalo in Ciranni

(2) moglie del Tenente Ciranni Sig. Carlo

Mellaha li 10 Ottobre 1931-IX

Il Capo

Il Colonnello A. A. Comandante della Aviazione (F. RANZA)

Firma del titolare — Firma dell' impiegato

(1) Ufficio cui è addetto l'impiegato. — (2) Qualifica dell'impiegato, o se trattasi di persona di famiglia, relazione di parentela o di servizio con l'impiegato, e nome e qualifica di questo.

Personal identification card released to the wife of a lieutenant from the airport of Mellaha, Libya.

Cat. R. A. n. 154

MINISTERO DELL'AERONAUTICA

AERONAUTICA A.O.

COMANDO SETTORE AERONAUTICO OVEST

Ufficio Demanio

TESSERA PERMANENTE DI RICONOSCIMENTO

rilasciata al Sig. (2) C. CICILIA Salvatore

il quale presta servizio in qualità di (3) Meccanico

presso il M.I.del Com:Sett: Aereo:Ovest Uff. Demanio.

ADDIS ABEBA / Marzo/193

IL CAPO UFFICIO

(Ten. Col. - Ing. Carlo Toscani)

Personal identification booklet released from the Eastern Africa Italian Air Force.

Mod. n. 90.
Regolam. sul Reclutam. (§ 936)
N. 34 del Catal. (R. 1921).

Corpo cui fu trasferito all'atto del congedamento (4) ....

Anno di nascita 1903

REGIA AERONAUTICA

(1) CENTRO AVIAZIONE DA CACCIA

FOGLIO DI CONGEDO ILLIMITATO

per (2) fine di ferma (Circ. 493 G.M. 1924)

che si rilascia a (3) Sorgno Giuseppe
Arrere

N.° di matricola (2) 55736 (41) il quale prende

domicilio nel Comune di Torino

Mandamento di Torino Distretto

militare di Torino

(6) Durante il tempo passato sotto le armi ha tenuto buona condotta ed ha servito con fedeltà ed onore

A Ghedi addì

Firma del Titolare (7) Giuseppe Sorgno

Il Comandante del Corpo
IL COMANDANTE DEL CENTRO
V. COMANDANTE DI STORMO
(A. Bosio)

Comune di Torino

Visto, addì 6. 10. 926

Il Sindaco

A 1924 dated Regia Aeronautica discharge document.

N. 69 catalogo R. A.

Repubblica Italiana

R. AERONAUTICA

COMANDO AERONAUTICA DELLA SICILIA

(1) CENTRO AFFLUENZA E RIORDINAMENTO

FOGLIO DI CONGEDO ILLIMITATO

per (2) Disp. Minist.

che si rilascia a (3) Av. gov. Randazzo Pasquale

classe 1923 Distretto di Leva Palermo N. di matric. (4)

il quale prende residenza nel Comune di Marineo

Provincia di Palermo

Circoscrizione del (5) Comando Aeronautica Sicilia in Palermo

(6)

A Palermo addì 16 Settembre 1947

FIRMA DEL TITOLARE IL COMANDANTE DEL (7)

COMUNE DI MARINEO

Visto, addì 17-9-947

IL CAPO DELL'AMMINISTRAZIONE COMUNALE

Regia Aeronautica discharge document.
Note there is no fasces (*fascio*) in the eagle's talons, however, the crowned eagle is the same style as during the war.

A humorous cartoon patriotic postcard depicting aerial acrobatics.

A humorous cartoon patriotic postcard.

A patriotic postcard from the Foggia Flight School.

This is a patriotic art postcard titled *Greetings to England*.

Axis and Allies (Rough) Air Force Rank Equivalents

Regia Aeronautica Italiana and *Deutsches Luftwaffe* (Rough) Rank Equivalents

Aviere:	Flieger
Aviere Scelto:	Gefreiter
Primo Aviere:	Obergefreiter
Aviere Capo:	Hauptgefreiter
Sergente:	Feldwebel
Sergente Maggiore:	Oberfeldwebel
Maresciallo 3A CL:	Fahnrich
Maresciallo 2A CL:	Oberfahnrich
Maresciallo 1A CL:	Stabsfeldwebel
Sottotenente:	Leutnant
Tenente:	Oberleutnant
Capitano:	Hauptmann
Maggiore:	Major
Tenente Colonnello:	Oberstleutnant
Colonnello:	Oberst
Generale di Brigata Aerea:	General Major
Generale di Divisione Aerea:	General Leutnant
Generale di Squadra Aerea:	General der Flieger
Generale d'Armata Aerea:	Generaloberst
Maresciallo dell'Aria:	Generalfeldmarschall

Regia Aeronautica Italiana and *British Royal Air Force* (Rough) Rank Equivalents

Aviere:	Aircraftsman 2nd Class
Aviere Scelto:	Aircraftsman 1st Class
Primo Aviere:	Leading Aircraftman
Aviere Capo:	Senior Aircraftsman
Sergente:	Sergeant
Sergente Maggiore:	Flight Sergeant
Maresciallo 3A CL:	—
Maresciallo 2ACL:	—
Maresciallo 1A CL:	Warrant Officer
Sottotenente:	Pilot Officer
Tenente:	Flying Officer
Capitano:	Flight Leiutenant
Maggiore:	Squadron Leader
Tenente Colonnello:	Wing Commander
Colonnello:	Group Captain
Generale di Brigata Aerea:	Air Commodore
Generale di Divisione Aerea:	Air Vice Marshal
Generale di Squadra Aerea:	Air Marshal
Generale d'Armata Aerea:	Air Chief Marshal
Maresciallo dell'Aria:	Marshal of the Royal Air Force

Regia Aeronautica Italiana and *United States Army Air Force* (Rough) Rank Equivalents

Aviere:	Private
Aviere Scelto:	Private 1st Class
Primo Aviere:	—
Aviere Capo:	—
Sergente:	Technical Sergeant
Sergente Maggiore:	Master Sergeant
Maresciallo 3A CL:	—
Maresciallo 2A CL:	Senior Officer Candidate
Maresciallo 1A CL:	Flight Officer
Sottotenente:	Second Lieutenant
Tenente:	First Lieutenant
Capitano:	Captain
Maggiore:	Major
Tenente Colonnello:	Lieutenant Colonel
Colonnello:	Colonel
Generale di Brigata Aerea:	Brigadier General
Generale di Divisione Aerea:	Major General
Generale di Squadra Aerea:	Lieutenant General
Generale d'Armata Aerea:	Four Star General
Maresciallo dell' Aria:	Five Star General

GLOSSARY

Aircraft radial engine: Motore Radiale
Airman/Airmen: Aviere/ Avieri
Aviator/ Aviators: Aviatore/ Aviatori

Badge: Fregio
Boots: Stivali

Cloak: Mantellina
Cockpit: Cabina di pilotaggio
Cowling: Cappottatura
Camoflage pattern: Schema mimetico

Fasces Emblem: Stemma con i fasci littori
First Model Flight Eagle: Aquila da pilota primo modello
Fleece collar: Collo di pelliccia
Flight suit: Tenuta di volo
Flight cap: Cuffia di volo
Flight Jacket: Giubbotto di volo
Forage cap: Berretto (or side cap/ Bustina)
Fuselage: Fusoliera

Goggles: Occhiali
Group: Gruppo

Landing gear: Carrello d'atterraggio

Machinegun: Mitragliatrice
Medal: Medaglia

Pants: Pantaloni
Parachute: Paracadute
Paratrooper: Paracadutista
Pistol: Pistola
Propeller: Elica

Ribbon: Nastrino
Roundel: Coccarda
Royal Air Force: Regia Aeronautica
Royal Air Force Eagle: Aquila della Regia Aeronautica

Star collar insignia: Stellette da bavero
Squadron: Squadriglia

Tail section: Sezione di coda (tail: coda)
Tropical helmet: Casco coloniale or casco tropicale
Tunic: Giacca

Visor cap: Cappello

Wing/ Wings: Ala/ali
White summer weight flight suit: Tenuta di volo bianca estiva

Further Reading

All Schiffer Military History Publications are highly recommended further reading sources!

Uniforms and Equipment of the Austro-Hungarian Army in World War One. Spencer A. Coil, Schiffer Publishing Ltd., Atglen, PA. 2003. 352 pages. This book contains black and white period images as well as a Color Gallery featuring flight badges.

Uniforms and Equipment of the Czarist Russian Armed Forces in World War I. Spencer Anthony Coil, Schiffer Publishing Ltd., Atglen, PA. 2005. 406 pages. This book contains black and white period images as well as a Color Gallery. There are images of aircraft and Cossacks.

Uniforms and Equipment of the French Armed Forces in World War I. Spencer Anthony Coil, Schiffer Publishing Ltd., Atglen, PA. 2005. 376 pages. This book contains black and white period images as well as a Color Gallery. There are many images of aircraft.

Uniforms and Equipment of the Italian Armed Forces in World War I. Spencer Anthony Coil, Schiffer Publishing Ltd., Atglen, PA. 2006. 432 pages. This book contains black and white period images as well as a Color Gallery. Use this book to see the evolution of the Italian armed forces since the First World War.

Uniforms and Equipment of the Central Powers in World War I: Austria-Hungary and Bulgaria. Spencer Anthony Coil, Schiffer Publishing Ltd., Atglen, PA. 2007. 376 pages. This book contains black and white period images as well as a Color Gallery. There are many images of aircraft.

Uniforms and Equipment of the Central Powers in World War I: Germany and Ottoman Turkey. Spencer Anthony Coil, Schiffer Publishing Ltd., Atglen, PA. 2007. 360 pages. This book contains black and white period images as well as a Color Gallery. There are many images of aircraft.

The German Wehrmacht on All Fronts 1939-1945: Volume One. Spencer Anthony Coil, Clemens Ellmauthaler, Schiffer Publishing Ltd., Atglen, PA. 2007. 296 pages. This book contains black and white period images all previously unpublished as well as a Color Gallery . This series can be used when comparing and contrasting Italian and German gear.

The German Wehrmacht on All Fronts 1939-1945: Volume Two. Spencer Anthony Coil, Clemens Ellmauthaler, Schiffer Publishing Ltd., Atglen, PA. 2008. 376 pages. This book contains black and white period images all previously unpublished as well as a Color Gallery. This series can be used when comparing and contrasting Italian and German gear.